WORLD BANK INDEPENDENT EVALUATION GROUP

IEG

Decentralization in Client Countries

An Evaluation of World Bank Support, 1990–2007

2008
The World Bank
Washington, D.C.

http://www.worldbank.org/ieg

1818 H Street NW
Washington, DC 20433
Telephone: 202-473-1000
Internet: www.worldbank.org
E-mail: feedback@worldbank.org

1 2 3 4 5 11 10 09 08

Cover: Village meeting in Ilha Ibo, Mozambique. ©Atlantide Phototravel/Corbis; reproduced by permission.

ISBN-13: 978-0-8213-7635-5
e-ISBN-13: 978-0-8213-7636-2
DOI: 10.1596/978-0-8213-7635-5

Library of Congress Cataloging-in-Publication data have been applied for.

World Bank InfoShop
E-mail: pic@worldbank.org
Telephone: 202-458-5454
Facsimile: 202-522-1500

Independent Evaluation Group
Knowledge Programs and Evaluation Capacity Development (IEGKE)
E-mail: eline@worldbank.org
Telephone: 202-458-4497
Facsimile: 202-522-3125

Printed on Recycled Paper

Contents

These appendixes are available online at
http://www.worldbank.org/ieg/decentralization/download.html

Abbreviations

CAE	Country Assistance Evaluation
CAO	Chief Accounting Officer
CAS	Country Assistance Strategy
CDD	Community-driven development
DAC	Development Assistance Committee (OECD)
DPL	Development Policy Loan
ESW	Economic and sector work
GFI	Government Financial Intermediary
HNP	Health, nutrition, and population
IADB	Inter-American Development Bank
ICR	Implementation Completion and Results Report
IEG	Independent Evaluation Group
IMF	International Monetary Fund
LGU	Local government unit
MDF	Municipal Development Fund
M&E	Monitoring and evaluation
OECD	Organisation for Economic Co-operation and Development
PFM	Public financial management
PREM	Poverty Reduction and Economic Management (Network)
PSAC	Programmatic Structural Adjustment Credit
UNCDF	United Nations Capital Development Fund
USAID	U.S. Agency for International Development
WDR	World Development Report

Grain storage huts, Mali. Photo courtesy of Kimberley Fletcher; FletcherGallery@Mac.com.

Acknowledgments

A team from the Country Evaluations and Regional Relations unit of the Independent Evaluation Group (IEG) team contributed to this report: Gita Gopal (task manager), Alisa Abrams, Tim L. de Vaan, Laurie Effron, Carolina Mary Rojas Hayes, Victor Orozco, Parameswaran Pramod, Rupa Ranganathan, Govinda Rao, Rohit Tharakan, Rajiv Tharian, Gemi Thomas, and Barbara Yale. Deanna Lijuaco, Arild Schou, Chil Soriano, and Germina Ssemogerere undertook field assessments in the Philippines and Uganda. Pierre M. De Raet and Manuel Penalver-Quesada participated in country missions. Jonathan Rodden prepared a background paper and contributed substantially to the evaluation in several ways.

The team acknowledges the technical guidance provided by Steven B. Webb and comments by Mark Sundberg, Victoria Elliot (former manager, IEG Corporate Evaluation and Methods), Martha Ainsworth, Dean Neilson, and Roy Gilbert. Toneema Haq and Svenja Weber-Venghaus prepared literature reviews on different aspects of decentralization and poverty reduction. The report was edited by Heather Dittbrenner and William B. Hurlbut. Vikki Taaka provided administrative guidance. The team is grateful for the guidance of Lily Chu (interim manager, Country Evaluations and Regional Relations) during the approach stage and that of the peer reviewers, Jennie Litvack and Ariel Fiszbein.

IEG acknowledges the cooperation and input of Patricia Clark Annez, Kai Kaiser, and Lili Liu, who collaborated with IEG in organizing four consultation meetings and contributed to the development of the evaluation design. IEG also acknowledges helpful input from Junaid Ahmad, William Dillinger, Matthew D. Glasser, Larry Hannah, Lance Morell, Amitaba Mukherjee, Harry Anthony Patrinos, Geeta Sethi, Mathew Verghis, Deborah Wetzel, and Roland White, and Inder Jit Ruprah, principal economist, Office of Evaluation and Oversight, of the Inter-American Development Bank. The team acknowledges the assistance of the task team leaders of the evaluated projects and economic and sector work. Comments on an earlier draft of this report from Andrew Reschovsky (professor, University of Wisconsin–Madison) and Joerg Faust (head of Department III: Governance, Statehood & Security, German Development Institute) are gratefully acknowledged.

IEG is grateful to the country directors and country teams, particularly lead staff on decentralization, in the countries where field visits were conducted. The country teams facilitated the visits and organized stakeholder consultation meetings. The IEG team also acknowledges the contribution of several World Bank client country stakeholders who provided feedback for the evaluation.

The evaluation was also informed by and benefited from several background papers on decentralization, the preparation of which was coordinated by Anwar Shah. These papers were prepared as part of a larger IEG effort to learn lessons of evaluation in improving public sector performance in developing countries. Six background papers were also prepared for this evaluation on Argentina (Erik Wibbels), Brazil (Jonathan Rodden), China (Jing Jin), India (Nirvikar Singh), Mexico (Alberto Diaz-Cayeros), and South Africa (Andrew Reschovsky). Their preparation was coordinated by Chad Leechor.

Director-General, Evaluation: *Vinod Thomas*
Director, Independent Evaluation Group–World Bank: *Cheryl W. Gray*
Senior Manager, IEGCR: *Ali M. Khadr*
Task Manager: *Gita Gopal*

Gathering in Bolivian village. Photo courtesy of World Bank Photo Library.

Foreword

Decentralization shifts responsibility and accountability for the delivery of public services to subnational (state, provincial, district, or local) levels of government, aiming to help improve service delivery and local governance. Since the 1990s, the World Bank has devoted an increasing share of its financing to support its client countries' decentralization efforts. To assess the results of such interventions, IEG reviewed Bank support for decentralization in 20 developing countries between fiscal years 1990 and 2007. This period had associated lending of about $22 billion, covering roughly half of all lending that included support for decentralization. IEG's evaluation did *not* attempt any systematic assessment of the costs and benefits of decentralization in client countries, noting that in many cases, the countries had made a political decision to decentralize well *before* requesting and receiving World Bank support.

According to the evaluation, Bank support for decentralization to the 20 focus countries was highly relevant. Most countries had embarked on a process to shift responsibilities for service delivery to subnational governments in areas such as primary education, basic health care, and water supply. World Bank support in these areas was responsive to client country demands, consistent with their development policies, and aligned with the institution's mandate of improving the delivery of basic services to the poor.

But the support for decentralization was of mixed quality, which nonetheless improved toward the end of the evaluation period, by which point it was rated high in about two-thirds of the focus countries. It was most successful in strengthening legal frameworks for decentralization and intergovernmental relations, improving public financial management at the local level, and helping central governments establish transparent fiscal transfer systems. It was much less successful in helping to enhance own-source revenue at the local levels, clarifying responsibilities of different levels of government, and strengthening citizen oversight.

The evaluation confirms that there is no single approach that can be considered in supporting decentralization across widely varying country situations. Solutions need to be tailored to country-specific contexts and driven by a commitment to reform at all levels of government. Even then, outcomes are sensitive to and positively associated with aspects such as subnational government capacity and political will.

That said, a number of directions emerge for seeking greater effectiveness of Bank support. One aspect concerns the need to ensure a cross-cutting understanding of the decentralization process, which will help to ensure consistent and coherent support across sector units. Another area of importance is each government's commitment to reform in this area, together with the need to strengthen capacity, including at local levels. Finally, it pays for countries to develop results-based frameworks to help assess the outcomes of reforms and the support for decentralization.

Vinod Thomas
Director-General, Evaluation

Local meeting in Indonesia. Photo by Ray Witlin, courtesy of the World Bank Photo Library.

Glossary

Administrative decentralization: The process of redistributing authority and responsibility for providing public services from the central or national level of government to a subnational and/or local level

"Big Bang" decentralization: A process wherein the central level of government announces decentralization; passes laws; and transfers responsibilities, authority, and/or staff to subnational and/or local governments in rapid succession

Decentralization: A process of transferring responsibility, authority, and accountability for specific or broad management functions to lower levels within an organization, system, or program (defined narrowly for purposes of this evaluation in chapter 1, box 1.1)

Decentralization framework: The full set of institutional arrangements in a given country within which decentralization is undertaken and sustained, specifying among other things how service delivery responsibilities and resource mobilization authority are apportioned among the various levels of government, as well as the associated accountability arrangements

Deconcentration: The least ambitious level of decentralization, where responsibilities are transferred to an administrative unit of the central government that is spatially closer to the population where service is to be provided, usually a field or regional office

Delegation: An intermediate level of decentralization, where some authority and responsibilities are transferred to a lower level of government, but there is a principal-agent relationship between the central and subnational government in question, with the agent remaining accountable to the principal

Devolution: The most ambitious form of decentralization, where the central government devolves responsibility, authority, and accountability to subnational governments with some degree of political autonomy

Fiscal decentralization: The decentralization of government expenditure and revenue-raising authority to subnational government structures in line with their allocated functional responsibilities

Horizontal decentralization: Delegation of decision-making powers, functions, and resources by a given level of government to other agencies, committees, and/or structures within the same level

Intergovernmental relations: Relations and accountability between different domains at a given level of government, as well as between different levels of government (for example, provincial-district)

Local government unit: The constitutionally established government structure that operates "closest" (in the sense of level, rather than space) to communities and is responsible for basic service delivery

Own-source revenue: Revenue from sources that have been assigned to a given subnational level of government, with the latter determining revenue rates

Political decentralization: A process whereby the voice of citizens is integrated into policy decisions at a subnational level and civil society can hold the associated authorities and officials accountable

Subnational government: A level of government below the national level; in federal systems, typically the level just below the central level

Strategy: The means employed to reach desired objectives, typically comprising such elements as clear policy underpinnings; an action plan based on lessons learned; a monitoring plan; and adequate financial, human, and technical resources for implementation

Vertical decentralization: Decentralization that occurs within sectors and departments but is not fully integrated and/or consistent with decentralization in other sectors and departments

Executive Summary

In recent years, developing countries have decentralized functions and responsibilities to lower levels of government at an increasing pace. The main reasons for such reforms are often political, but governments also adopt them as a way to improve service delivery and local governance. Typically, after the political decision is made, a country will turn to its development partners—including the World Bank—for support in implementing the new policies and achieving their development objectives.

The Independent Evaluation Group (IEG) assessed the effectiveness of Bank support for decentralization between fiscal 1990 and 2007 in 20 countries, seeking to inform the design and implementation of future support. Given the difficulties of measuring the results of decentralization, the evaluation used intermediate outcome indicators—such as strengthened legal and regulatory frameworks for intergovernmental relations, improved administrative capacity, and increased accountability of subnational governments and functionaries to higher levels of government and to citizens—to assess the results of Bank support in these 20 countries. To examine potential lessons at a sectoral level, the evaluation also assessed whether Bank support for decentralization improved intermediate outcomes for service delivery in the education sector in 6 of the 20 countries.

Bank support contributed to more effective decentralization—substantially in more than one-third of the 20 cases and modestly in the others. The most successful aspects of Bank support pertained to the legal frameworks for intergovernmental relations, the frameworks for intergovernmental fiscal transfers, and subnational financial management. Bank support was less effective in clarifying the roles and responsibilities of different levels of government and in improving own-source revenue mobilization by subnational governments. This was often a result of lack of political will.

Other things being equal, Bank support brought better results where there was consensus around the reform within the country prior to Bank engagement and when the support was combined with incentives for institutional reform at the subnational level. Looking forward, the results of Bank support for decentralization can be strengthened with more timely and coordinated analytical work to underpin it, by better coordinating fragmented sector-by-sector interventions, and by accompanying support for policy reform with technical assistance to strengthen local government capacity.

Introduction

All 20 countries reviewed in this evaluation have devolved significant responsibilities to lower levels of government. Politics may be behind this trend, fueled by a desire among citizens for strengthened democracy and improved governance and service delivery. But both the emergence of strong urban economies and ethnic tensions that threaten national identities also motivate governments to move closer to the people. Governments have not usually asked the World Bank to help with their decisions about whether to decentralize, nor has the Bank typically advocated decentralization, except in particular sectors. Usually—in 12 of the 20 case-study countries—governments have decentralized for political reasons and only subsequently asked the Bank to help implement the process, make it more rational, and improve service delivery and accountability.

Objectives of the evaluation

IEG assessed the effectiveness of Bank support for decentralization provided to 20 countries between fiscal 1990 and 2007. These countries were selected to ensure regional representation, and they accounted for 47 percent of all Bank commitments containing decentralization components during the period. The aim was to examine what worked and what did not to inform the design and implementation of future Bank support.

Decentralization has many meanings, but for this evaluation it was defined as *the transfer of authority and responsibility for governance and public service delivery from a higher to a lower level of government.* The characteristic that distinguishes decentralization from, say, simply shifting resources to local governments is that decentralization seeks to create relationships of accountability among citizens, service providers, and subnational governments and between the latter and central governments. The evaluation does not assess community-driven development, which was assessed in a separate IEG evaluation (2005b).

The evaluation framework

It has yet to be conclusively demonstrated that there is a causal link between decentralization and improved service delivery, good governance, or macroeconomic stabilization. Moreover, decentralization is a long-term agenda—industrialized countries often took more than a century to reach their current state of decentralization, and one or two Bank country strategy periods are simply inadequate to assess that. The decentralization process is also typically disjointed and subject to periods of progress and reversal. Therefore, rather than focus on the whole decentralization process or the connections between decentralization and service delivery, IEG focused on a set of intermediate outcomes that are essential for good service delivery in decentralized settings.

The key desired result is fiscally responsible, responsive, and accountable subnational governments that are likely, under the oversight of citizens and higher-level government, to improve service delivery and governance. The desired result has several components:

Figure ES.1: Framework for Assessing the Results of Bank Support for Decentralization

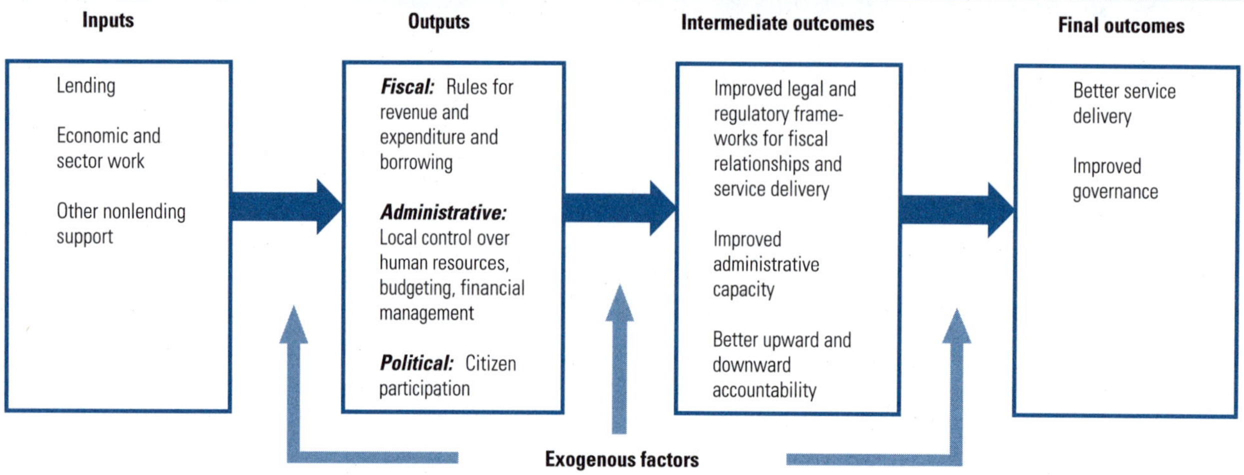

Source: IEG.

- Strengthened legal and regulatory frameworks for intergovernmental relations
- Improved administrative capacity
- Increased accountability of subnational governments and functionaries to higher levels of government and to local citizens.

IEG assessed the extent to which Bank support contributed to progress toward these objectives from 1990 to 2007. At the sectoral level, the evaluation assessed the extent to which Bank support in the education sector in 6 of the 20 focus countries helped generate resources for local governments to deliver services (consistent with formal intergovernmental fiscal frameworks), strengthened institutions and capacity for improved service delivery, and enhanced the accountability of local governments for service delivery to citizens.

Evaluation Findings

Quality of Bank support

To understand the quality of Bank support, the evaluation reviewed all Country Assistance Strategies in the 20 countries, more than 40 pieces of relevant economic and sector work, and 203 lending activities with decentralization components. The 203 lending activities in these countries had associated financial commitments of about $22 billion, of which about $7.4 billion was specifically for decentralization-related activities.

The quality of Bank economic and sector work on decentralization was mixed during the 1990s. The work was not always timely and in several countries did not influence the design of Bank Country Assistance Strategies. Of the 20 country cases studied for this evaluation, decentralization-related diagnostic reports existed in 16. Only in 8 was timely analysis of the implications of decentralization policy undertaken within five years of issuance of the relevant laws. The evaluation also found little evidence that broader analytical work on decentralization had substantial influence on Bank operations in the countries studied. Sound analysis, when it was done, tended to affect assistance from the same Bank sector unit that undertook the analysis, but not usually beyond.

The quality of the Bank's lending portfolio to these 20 countries was also mixed during the 1990s. Weak understanding of political economy factors and associated risks led to overly ambitious objectives that often limited development effectiveness. Bank support for decentralization was provided by various sector units, with objectives that were not always consistent at the country level. Bank support focused on decentralization frameworks, but did not always provide parallel support to strengthen the technical capacity of the subnational governments to whom responsibilities and resources were transferred. Monitoring of the progress of Bank support for decentralization was weak; the Bank focused on output- or process-level indicators, such as the passage of laws or fiscal transfers, rather than on the performance of local governments and other institutions in delivering services.

In the last five years of the evaluation period, the quality of Bank support for decentralization improved in 15 of the 20 countries. Bank analytical work provided a better understanding of the broader implications of decentralization for service delivery and governance and in turn influenced the design of country strategies. Country-level assistance was therefore internally more consistent.

In several countries, support for policy reform was combined with technical assistance to strengthen different levels of government, and the Bank increasingly supported country efforts to assess the results of decentralization in terms of strengthened local government performance. Donor collaboration also improved during this period, and in several of the 20 countries joint diagnostic and analytical work—including at subnational levels—led to joint support for decentralization.

This said, the organizational structure within the Bank has in general resulted in less-than-optimum support for decentralization at the country level. An absence of clear leadership and coordination across sectors persists, except in a handful of cases where country directors and/or vice presidents have broken the sector-silo approach, thereby enabling more consistent support to client countries.

Results of Bank support

The evaluation divided the review of the results of Bank support for decentralization into two parts: support for the development and/or strengthening of decentralization frameworks, and support for improving service delivery in the education sector.

In supporting the development and/or strengthening of decentralization frameworks, the Bank generated outcomes that were high or substantial in 7 countries, modest in 12, and negligible in 1. Bank support for decentralization was most successful in helping strengthen the legal underpinnings of intergovernmental fiscal relations. The Bank helped establish frameworks for prudent borrowing and debt management, generating substantial results in half the countries to which it provided support. Support for strengthening financial accountability of subnational governments to higher levels of government also generated substantial results. The Bank was less successful in helping to strengthen frameworks for own-source revenue or in enhancing such revenue; it contributed to substantial and sustained results in only five countries. The Bank also was not very successful in helping clarify the responsibilities of the various levels of government or in supporting monitoring at the local level.

The Bank contributed to better results in countries where the political will to decentralize was strong, where there was greater clarity on the type of fiscal and administrative decentralization to be pursued, and where Bank support was aligned with the client's decentralization strategy. This was the case notably in two post-conflict countries, where consensus on the need to minimize the potential for conflict was compelling. In countries where there was less consensus on the approach to implementing fiscal or administrative decentralization, the results of Bank support were weaker. This was often because the Bank supported approaches that were inconsistent with client country objectives.

The evaluation reviewed Bank support for decentralization in the education sector in greater depth in 6 of the 20 focus countries (there are ongoing evaluations in health, water, and municipal management). The evaluation found that sector-level efforts to decentralize education services were not usually sustained or effective unless they were designed and implemented at the country level within a broad decentralization framework.

The evaluation did not attempt to aggregate ratings of the quality of Bank support or ratings of the results of Bank support for decentralization frameworks into a single rating for each of the 20 countries. However, a comparison of the ratings for quality and results indicates that when the quality of Bank support improves, the results also get better. This suggests that closer monitoring of the quality of Bank support for decentralization will likely improve the Bank's contribution to overall results in the country.

Recommendations

In many of its country programs, the Bank has made a de facto strategic decision to support decentralization and development of subnational government capacity. In a few cases—such as where the client country has made decentralization a cornerstone of its development strategy and has demonstrated political commitment to decentralizing—Bank support has been built on an explicitly cross-cutting approach. In most cases, however, Bank support has taken a sector-specific route, targeting decentralization and/or development of subnational government capacity as a logical way of supporting more effective and responsive service delivery in that sector. In these latter cases, the various Bank sector units have not always provided consistent or coherent support for decentralization.

Looking forward, IEG offers the following recommendations. They are applicable to every client country that has transferred at least some responsibility for service delivery to subnational governments, where the Bank has made a de facto strategic decision to provide support for decentralization through either a cross-cutting or a sector-specific approach:

- Ensure that Bank support—particularly lending—is underpinned by genuine client commitment to decentralized service delivery, given its importance to the success of Bank interventions. Occasionally, a role for the Bank may be justified in the absence of client commitment (for example, to forestall potentially adverse measures), although the evaluation finds that Bank interventions under such circumstances are not usually effective.
- Encourage the adoption of a more results-based approach to decentralization by helping develop in-country and Bank capacity for monitoring and evaluation that focuses on local outcomes (such as enhanced accountability, greater citizen participation, and improved service delivery) rather than on just the process of decentralization.
- Ensure that Bank support at the country level is (among other things):
  - Founded on a clear analytical framework based on an integrative understanding of economic, political, and institutional factors at different levels of government and across sectors affected by decentralization
  - Accompanied by support (from the Bank or others) to develop and maintain local government capacity, to the extent feasible.
- Strengthen institutional arrangements within the Bank to ensure that an integrative view underpins Bank interventions, particularly those based on sector-specific entry points.

Village meeting in Indonesia. Photo by Ray Witlin, courtesy of the World Bank Photo Library.

Management Response

Management welcomes the Independent Evaluation Group (IEG) evaluation of World Bank support for decentralization, covering engagement in 20 client countries and operations between 1990 and 2007. Management broadly concurs with the review's recommendations, although these require some nuance and clarification; subject to these, management intends to build on the review's findings in its work in supporting countries that ask for assistance on decentralization.

Concurrence with the Broad Thrust of the Analysis and Recommendations

The evaluation contains important conclusions that management welcomes in the context of its overall assistance to countries on decentralization and improved service delivery. Management recognizes that an evaluation of decentralization was from the outset likely to be challenging, given its cross-cutting and often politically driven nature. Management appreciates the finding that Bank support in this area has improved notably over the latter period of the evaluation. We broadly welcome a number of the recommendations that can further support this trend going forward. We welcome the overall thrust of the evaluation that engagement on decentralization should reflect the prevailing client country context, to support development results. We also appreciate the overall tone of the evaluation, which suggests that in general the Bank has not acted as an "ideological" proponent of decentralization, but has sought to support decentralization as an intermediate means to improve service delivery and poverty reduction. Management has only a few issues to raise with regard to the analysis in the review.

Management Observations

Management's observations center on three issues: (i) the objectives for Bank engagement with partner countries in supporting their decentralization efforts, (ii) support for countries' monitoring of decentralization efforts and evaluation of results, and (iii) support for strengthening local governments.

Objectives for Bank engagement with decentralization and attribution

Management embraces the report's emphasis on improving service delivery as the ultimate objective of our involvement with decentralization. Our work on decentralization per se will be driven by this goal. Management recognizes that, with regard to decentralization, as with virtually all types of support, alignment of Bank engagement with country commitment is central to achieving sustainable development results. However, management notes that decentralization has not proven to be either a necessary or a sufficient condition for good service delivery. Nor is there any necessary link between a client's intention to decentralize government and a primary commitment to improve service delivery, which may often be driven by other (valid) political objectives. Thus, our engagement on helping countries improve service delivery must be guided by our judgment of the best steps toward achieving that goal, taking into account government commitment on a host of issues that affect it, including decentralization.

Monitoring and evaluation of decentralized results

Management is very much in accord with the recommendation to help partner countries monitor results more carefully. Management emphasizes that measurement should be extended to assessing outcomes in terms of improved service delivery. Measurement of both of these elements would permit a much-needed assessment of the actual transmission mechanism between adherence to basic and very broadly defined principles of public finance/ public sector reform and governance (such as enhanced citizen accountability) and actual improvements in much-needed services. Such discipline is needed to ensure that intermediate instruments are ultimately assessed for their impact on outcomes. Furthermore, the Bank needs to work closely with client counterparts to ensure that monitoring systems are themselves sustainable and to measure impacts over longer periods of time, given that decentralization reforms may be subject to significant lags. Beyond measurement, the Bank can assist client countries in designing feasible impact assessment strategies for decentralization measures.

Support for strengthening local government

Management is encouraged that the report notes recent progress in taking an integrative, multidisciplinary approach to assisting countries that are grappling with the decentralization of their governments. Management intends to continue to reinforce and broaden this trend, while recognizing that each country's experience in this area is necessarily unique. Our strategies must accordingly reflect this diversity, and management must, in partnership with client countries, develop a vision of intermediate goals that may emphasize some sectors more than others in different phases. Management shares the goal of improving capacity in local governments but notes its emphasis on "as needed to improve local service delivery," and it will design its support to encourage this. However, management does not subscribe to the notion that the only—or best—means of achieving capacity goals is through direct support to local governments from the World Bank or others, especially because it risks being supply driven. Consequently, engagement in decentralization must pay particular attention to effective and incentive-compatible efforts to strengthen local governments, for example, through support linked to performance (including on intermediate process indicators and final outcomes). Management also notes that the Bank's recent Governance and Anti-Corruption Strategy (World Bank 2007e) encourages governments to explore demand-side accountability, including citizen oversight. Management has already committed to report back to the Board on the implementation of this strategy.

Conclusion

Overall, management welcomes this evaluation from IEG and broadly accepts its recommendations. Detailed responses to the recommendations are outlined in the Management Action Record.

Management Action Record

IEG Recommendation	Management Response
Ensure that Bank support—particularly lending—is underpinned by genuine client commitment to decentralized service delivery, given its importance to the success of Bank interventions. Occasionally, a role for the Bank may be justified in the absence of client commitment (for example, to forestall potentially adverse measures), although the evaluation finds that Bank interventions under such circumstances are not usually effective.	***Ongoing/Agreed in Principle.*** Management agrees in principle with this recommendation; however, it notes that the degree of country consensus around appropriate decentralization modalities may differ by sectors and levels of government. Consequently, the Bank can often play a critical role helping countries identify and implement entry points intended to promote quality in decentralized service delivery. However, a number of cases suggest that political drivers for decentralization are often an important country dynamic, and Bank country strategy design and implementation must be responsive to these realities. Management agrees to continue to emphasize cross-cutting client commitment for decentralized service delivery as a critical factor in defining entry points for successful engagement, and to calibrate assistance to support sustainable service delivery and poverty reduction as good practice in relevant Country Assistance Strategy (CAS) design and implementation. To implement the Governance and Anti-Corruption (GAC) Strategy, the Bank's Regional vice presidential units have identified 26 countries that are initiating country-specific GAC processes. Where country conditions involve significant issues of decentralized service delivery (for example, the Democratic Republic of Congo, Indonesia, and the Philippines), country teams are systematically deepening the analysis around political-economy circumstances in shaping development effectiveness. At the conclusion of this learning process, Bank management is committed to reporting to the Board whether and how it intends to systematize and scale up its GAC work, including analytic and advisory activities. Reporting on the above agreed actions will be done in the context of overall GAC reporting.
Encourage the adoption of a more results-based approach to decentralization by helping to develop in-country and Bank capacity for monitoring and evaluation (M&E) that focuses on local outcomes (such as enhanced accountability, greater citizen participation, and improved service delivery) rather than on just the process of decentralization.	***Ongoing/Agreed.*** The Bank will continue to place particular emphasis in its dialogue with client countries on supporting the existence of a credible data-collection and reporting system for relevant services, one that is consistent with the structure of decentralization both in terms of its level of aggregation and management responsibilities and that can be used to make midcourse corrections as needed. At the same time, the design of M&E systems needs to highlight the presumed results chains between intermediate outcomes and ultimate outcomes (service delivery). For operations supporting a broad-based engagement in decentralized outcomes, countries will be encouraged to adopt a system that reflects the M&E system in place at the national level.

Management Action Record

IEG Recommendation	Management Response
	At the national level, the Public Expenditure and Financial Accountability (PEFA) 8 indicators (concerning intergovernmental fiscal relations) and the PEFA 23 indicators (concerning front-line school and health facility financing) provide for systematic assessments of intermediate outcomes. The PEFA Secretariat also recently issued guidance on subnational government applications of this public financial management diagnostic tool, useful to countries to consider for M&E at this level. As part of the GAC Implementation Plan, management has committed to strengthen the application of Actionable Governance Indicators, including those in the area of decentralization. Management will continue its efforts to provide country and individual operations teams with guidance on helping countries strengthen M&E around decentralization.
Ensure that Bank support at the country level is (among other things): • Founded on a clear analytical framework based on an integrative understanding of economic, political, and institutional factors at different levels of government and across sectors affected by decentralization • Accompanied by support (from the Bank or others) to develop and maintain local government capacity to the extent feasible.	***Ongoing/Agreed in Part.*** Given the cross-cutting nature of decentralization, management agrees that an integrated approach is important as part of general and specialized economic and sector work, including attention to the political-economy of decentralization (for example, Public Expenditure Reviews and sectoral diagnostics, including around GAC issues). Management agrees with the first part of this recommendation and will implement it and monitor progress in the context of the GAC work noted in its response to the first recommendation. Management agrees that support for subnational capacity can be a vital ingredient to strengthening service delivery outcomes. However, management notes that strengthening government capacity must be linked to ultimate service delivery outcomes and based on appropriate engagement models and Bank comparative advantage, especially in the presence of a large number of diverse subnational jurisdictions. Local capacity building cannot be limited to, for example, the supply of training, but depends on appropriate incentives. Experience shows that it must be demand driven to be effective. Although strengthening local capacity often represents an important element for effective decentralization, management does not commit to always supplying local capacity building as an element in the activities it supports.

Management Action Record

IEG Recommendation	Management Response
Strengthen institutional arrangements within the Bank to ensure that an integrative view underpins Bank interventions, particularly those based on sector-specific entry points.	***Ongoing/Agreed.*** Management underscores the role of country management units and Regional vice presidential units (with support from multisectoral communities of practice in the Regions) in ensuring that consistent approaches are implemented as part of the CASs and operational review processes. Management will ensure that the issue is raised early in relevant CAS discussions. At a Bank-wide level, the Decentralization and Sub-National Regional Economics Thematic Group will continue to serve as a platform to promote integrative approaches to strengthen results-based decentralization engagements, working together with other related cross-cutting thematic groups, notably the Urban Economics, Finance, and Management Thematic Group. Within the Bank-wide initiative to revitalize and support communities of practice, management sees this as a cross-network area to prioritize. This work will facilitate coordination across networks/sector teams at the Regional level. To support coherent approaches, the thematic group structure will offer senior facilitation and advisory services on a demand basis to country teams engaged in upstream CAS or project design issues. Specific steps to strengthen Bank engagement on issues of decentralization and local governance are under preparation under the guidance of senior operational management.

Meeting on women's role in society, Dushanbe, Tajikistan. Photo by Gennadiy Ratushenko, courtesy of the World Bank Photo Library.

Chairperson's Summary: Committee on Development Effectiveness (CODE)

On May 21, 2008, the Committee on Development Effectiveness (CODE) discussed the "Evaluation of Bank Support for Decentralization in Client Countries" and the draft management response.

Background

Key strategy documents include *Strengthening World Bank Group Engagement on Governance and Anticorruption* (World Bank 2007l) and *Reforming Public Institutions and Strengthening Governance: A World Bank Strategy* (World Bank 2000c). The updates on the implementation of the 2000 Bank strategy were prepared in 2002 and 2005 as part of the "Sector Strategy Implementation Update: FY05" (World Bank 2005g), which was discussed by CODE. Related Independent Evaluation Group (IEG) evaluations include the recent *Public Sector Reform: What Works and Why?* (IEG 2008), considered by CODE in March 2008.

Main Findings and Recommendations

IEG assessed the effectiveness of Bank support for decentralization between fiscal 1990 and 2007 in 20 countries, seeking to inform the design and implementation of future support. The evaluation also assessed the results of Bank support for decentralization of service delivery in the education sector. IEG found that the most successful aspects of Bank support pertained to the frameworks for intergovernmental relations including fiscal transfers and subnational financial management. Bank support was less effective in clarifying the roles and responsibilities of different levels of government and in improving their own-source revenue mobilization. Looking ahead, IEG makes the following recommendations: (i) ensure that Bank support is grounded in genuine client commitment to decentralized service delivery; (ii) encourage a more results-based approach by helping to develop in-country and Bank capacity for monitoring and evaluation that focuses on local outcomes; (iii) ensure that Bank support is based on a clear analytical framework, accompanied by strengthening of local government capacity; and (iv) strengthen institutional arrangements within the Bank to ensure that an integrated view underpins Bank interventions, particularly those based on sector-specific entry points.

Draft management response

Although concurring with the broad thrust of the analysis and recommendations, management commented on three issues: (i) the objectives of the Bank's engagement with partner countries in supporting their decentralization efforts, which is centered on helping improve service delivery; (ii) support for countries' monitoring and evaluation systems; and (iii) support for strengthening local governments, where it notes the importance of incentives and demand-driven approaches.

DGE statement

In his statement, the Director-General, Evaluation (DGE) noted a few challenges specific to this evaluation: the consequent need to formulate an operative definition, an absence of a specific articulated sector/thematic strategy, and the long-term nature of the process. Accordingly, the evaluation needed to be based on intermediate outcome indicators. The DGE highlighted three key lessons from the evaluation: (i) Bank support for decentralization is highly relevant, (ii) Bank support to decentralization should be tailored to varying country contexts, and (iii) results of Bank support have been better when such support was framed around a country-led strategy.

Overall Conclusions and Next Steps

The Committee welcomed the opportunity to discuss the IEG evaluation. CODE found the management response to be constructive, accepting, and appreciative of IEG's findings and recommendations. A few speakers wondered whether in such instances of substantive entente there was any value added in holding a CODE discussion. Other members disagreed, because of the strategic salience of the topic and the need for an independent validation of confirmation of what the Bank was or was not doing. Some speakers expressed their disappointment with (i) the overly narrow definition employed, focusing on service delivery; (ii) neglect of the whole cost side of decentralization and, more broadly, of its sustainability, noting in particular aspects such as fiscal costs, coordination failures, administrative duplication, and distributional consequences. Relatedly, a few other speakers wondered whether the Bank's efforts (and hence the evaluation) were not sidestepping the key policy debates and suggested it could be more ambitious in helping client countries think through the options. There was broad endorsement of the recommendation on client commitment and political will, although a cautionary note was expressed regarding the complexity of the issue and attendant nuances in reading the messages. There was overall consensus among the speakers that decentralization is a means and not the objective per se; it is a country-driven process and the Bank should play a supportive, demand-driven role in it. In this regard, it was noted that understanding the political economy of the decentralization context is important. The findings and recommendations (accepted and indeed elaborated on by management) regarding institutional fragmentation and the need for increased coherence and integration across sectors resonated with many speakers.

The following main issues were raised.

Notion of decentralization and scope of evaluation

Speakers expressed divergent views about the notion of decentralization and the scope of the IEG evaluation. Some members felt that limiting the notion of decentralization to service delivery was misleading. *IEG responded that the subject for evaluation had been narrowed intentionally because the service delivery element was the critical one for poverty reduction and a major element underlying intergovernmental relations.* A member noted that the decentralization process always involved costs (for example, fiscal, administrative, and costs of coordination failures and income distribution). To this end, members suggested measuring the efficiency of decentralization by costs and benefits as well as by its contribution to effective public service delivery. In this regard, speakers expressed a preference to include in the evaluation an analysis of costs and benefits of decentralization. A member suggested addressing the cost side in the Public Expenditure Reviews. *IEG responded that chapter 3 of the report partially covered the cost side by describing the fiscal costs and the potential macrostabilization issues. At the same time, IEG noted that (i) the evaluation intended to assess the outcome of Bank support for decentralization, not to weigh costs and benefits of decentralization; (ii) costs and benefits had a number of dimensions that were beyond the Bank's mandate and were political or quasipolitical in nature; and (iii) it was difficult to capture all dimensions of costs and benefits. Management agreed to adopt a more systemic approach to reviewing Public Expenditure Reviews, especially when they include analysis of the fiscal costs of decentralization.*

Other speakers broadly agreed with the thrust of IEG's recommendations and appreciated the constructive draft management response. They found this evaluation to be very strong and noted that decentralization is a new approach to development. Members agreed that decentralization was just a tool that could serve different purposes, including but not limited to improving public service delivery. In this context, a member preferred the term "intergovernmental relationships" to the term "decentralization." A speaker noted that promoting spatial planning and regional development is an important objective of decentralization and appreciated some indications from IEG on the relevance of this objective for the Bank's work.

Focus of Bank's support for decentralization

Although welcoming IEG's finding about improved quality of Bank support for decentralization, some members suggested that the Bank be more ambitious in encouraging countries' decentralization efforts where it is appropriate and contributing to policy debates, particularly in the small and fragile states. They recommended enhancing Bank support by sharing best practice. *IEG broadly agreed with this recommendation but stressed the importance of proceeding with caution, given that decentralization in many countries (including several small states) reflected deeply held political beliefs about its value.* Some speakers encouraged the Bank to play an advisory role and focus more on analytical work and technical assistance. A speaker sought more information about the appropriate staff skill mix to effectively support decentralization efforts in client countries.

Country context

Members agreed that country specifics should be taken into account. A speaker emphasized the importance of understanding which factors drive the decentralization agenda. The need for studying a country's political economy was reiterated. A member suggested discussing and analyzing the final outcomes of decentralization in countries. Some speakers felt that decentralization is the right option for the African countries. One member was not certain about the findings of IEG that Bank support is weak when it is inconsistent with the government view and that it is successful in the countries with existing political will. He noted that there is no clear concept of political will as far as decentralization is concerned. In this context, another member remarked that the level of decentralization often depends on the central government's decisions and, hence, decentralization has a very political nature.

Development capacity at the local level

A member was concerned about IEG's recommendation to develop the capacity of local governments. He noted that Bank clients are central governments and did not believe that the Bank's engagement at the local level would have a significant impact. In this regard, some speakers underlined that such engagement should be demand driven. *Both IEG and management agreed with the need for Bank involvement at the local level to be demand driven.* A member sought clarification from management about whether the development of local capacity was an issue of incentives or training. *Management noted that both aspects are important; however, experience shows that training needs to be demand driven.*

Coherence in the Bank's advice

Speakers took note of the IEG finding about the existing fragmentation within the Bank in providing support to decentralization. They emphasized the importance of consistent Bank advice to client countries and requested information on the specific actions aimed at ensuring internal collaboration and avoiding fragmentation be included in the Management Action Record relating to the report. *Management explained that the Bank did not find it desirable to establish one central unit to coordinate all work. At the same time, management implements specific actions to improve coherence in three areas: (i) at the country level, through strengthening upstream diagnostic, embedding decentralization agenda in Country Assistance Strategies/Country Partnership Strategies, and the existing Anchor Groups in SD, HD, and PREM; (ii) at the central level, through cross-cutting thematic groups such as those on decentralization and urban economics, finance, and management; and (iii) at the Bank-wide level, through the Governance Council.* A member asked about the additional costs of ensuring coherence. *Management clarified that this is not a major resource issue.*

Donor harmonization

Some members stressed the need for donor collaboration and harmonization for effective partnerships with client countries. *Management clarified that the Bank is actively involved in the harmonization process through the Development Partners Group on Local Governance and Decentralization that is informally aligned with the Organisation for Economic Co-operation and Development-Development Assistance Committee.*

Globalization and localization

A member suggested looking at decentralization from both globalization and localization perspectives (that is, applying both top-down and bottom-up approaches for analysis and evaluation). He said that in many countries, the decentralization process comes as a reaction of the central government to bottom-up requests and development and asked IEG to take this into account for future evaluations. The importance of applying the notion of subsidiarity to decentralization was also emphasized in this context.

Jiayi Zou, Chairperson

Chapter 1

Evaluation Essentials

- Countries have increasingly adopted decentralized forms of governance and have turned to the Bank for support in their efforts.
- Potential gains from decentralization can include enhanced government accountability and more effective and efficient service delivery.
- Risks associated with decentralization include macroeconomic instability, corruption, and elite capture.
- In assessing intermediate outcomes in 20 countries from fiscal 1990 to fiscal 2007, IEG included the quality of intergovernmental fiscal frameworks, subnational institutions and administrative capacity, and accountability of subnational governments.

Multipurpose Hall in Sri Lankan village. Photo by Dominic Sansoni, courtesy of the World Bank Photo Library.

Background and Objectives

Countries have been turning to the World Bank for support with decentralization for more than two decades. Beginning in the 1980s, and with a marked increase in pace and scale beginning around the mid-1990s, the Bank has provided some form of lending and nonlending support to 89 client countries.

This evaluation, which covers the period fiscal 1990 to 2007, assesses the quality and results of that support in 20 of those 89 countries where support was most substantial in terms of World Bank financing (the support to these 20 countries represents about 47 percent of total Bank financial support for decentralization during the evaluation period). A key aim of the evaluation is to draw lessons for future Bank support for decentralization.

Decentralization is the transfer of administrative and financial authority and responsibility for governance and public service delivery from a higher level of government to a lower level. The precise dimension (or ambition), appellation, level of responsibility, and set of government authorities involved has varied widely by country. In terms of general patterns, however, the development literature identifies three dimensions and three modes of decentralization (box 1.1). This evaluation seeks to cover all three dimensions and modes.

Literature Review: Arguments for and against Decentralization and Findings from Empirical Studies

Although political arguments in favor of decentralization have been advanced for several centuries, the emphasis more recently has been on economic arguments. Development agencies, among others, have tended to focus on the benefits of decentralization for service delivery based on the principle of subsidiarity[1] (Shah 1998; Litvack and Seddon 1999; Manor 2003; World Bank 1997b, 2004j; Ahmad and others 2005; and Shah 2006b). The focus has been primarily on fiscal decentralization, with the goal of improving allocative efficiency by bringing citizens closer to decision making and giving them the chance to prioritize the use of public resources. Such fiscal decentralization can also, under certain conditions, strengthen accountability, because citizen participation, monitoring, and control of local governments are relatively easier at the local level (OECD-DAC 2004).

Recent arguments for decentralization focus on efficient service delivery.

The 2004 *World Development Report: Making Services Work for Poor People* (World Bank 2004j) notes that decentralization is one institutional mechanism that is often proposed to improve service delivery. It adds that experience with the use of this mechanism has varied and has produced mixed results. The World Development Report (WDR) notes that in Bolivia the creation of rural local governments was associ-

Box 1.1: What Is Decentralization?

Dimensions	Modes
Administrative decentralization—How responsibilities and authorities for policies and decisions are shared between levels of government and how these are turned into allocative outcomes	*Devolution*—The deepest form of decentralization, in which a government devolves responsibility, authority, and accountability to lower levels with some degree of political autonomy
Fiscal decentralization—The assignment of expenditures, revenues (transfers and/or revenue-raising authority), and borrowing among different levels of governments	*Delegation*—Some authority and responsibilities transferred, but with a principal-agent relationship between the central and lower levels of government, with the agent remaining accountable to the principal
Political decentralization—How the voice of citizens is integrated into policy decisions and how civil society can hold authorities and officials accountable at different levels of government	*Deconcentration*—The shallowest form of decentralization, in which responsibilities are transferred to an administrative unit of the central government, usually a field, regional, or municipal office

Source: IEG staff.

ated with dramatic shifts in public allocations away from infrastructure and into social sectors—and a sharp fall in the geographic concentration of public investments as they become more evenly dispersed across regions (Faguet 2001). In some other countries, in contrast, decentralization has led to increased regional inequalities and the "capture" of public resources by local elites.

Case studies at a sectoral level also do not lead to any firm conclusions about the benefits of decentralization. Some case studies in the health sector have found that decentralization has had negative effects on the quality of service delivery. Lakshminarayanan (2003) found that devolution in the Philippines disrupted the integrity of the referral chain related to the delivery of services such as emergency obstetric care. In Zambia and again in the Philippines, Aitken (1998) found that changes in salary levels, inadequate funding of local health programs, and the politicization of local appointments increased uncertainty and led to deterioration in staff morale and quality of care.

Research has found weaker connections between decentralization and service delivery in health but stronger connections in education.

In the education sector, in contrast, case studies have generally found positive results from decentralization, particularly where local communities became involved. In a survey of international experience, Winkler and Gershberg (2000) found good outcomes associated with increased local autonomy, although they also found significant impediments to realizing the potential from decentralization in some countries. Studies have also found that increasing parents' participation in community-managed schools led to significantly lower rates of student and teacher absenteeism in El Salvador (Jimenez and Sawada 1999); that decentralization improved students' test scores in Argentina (Galiani and Schargrodsky 2001; Eskeland and Filmer 2002); and that decentralized management of schools led to improved achievement scores in Nicaragua (King and Ozler 1998).

The literature also highlights risks associated with decentralization when local capacity, accountability, and institutions are weak. The 1997 WDR (World Bank 1997b) warns of the risk of macroeconomic instability caused by weakened fiscal discipline under decentralization. Poor local implementation capacity can lead to increased inefficiency and waste in service delivery (Bird, Ebel, and Wallich 1995; Prud'homme 1995; and Tanzi 1996). In addition, capture by political and other local elites can readily emerge as power is transferred to the local level, where entrenched inequities may help elites orient service delivery toward themselves and away from the poor (Jette 2005; Manor 2003; OECD-DAC 2004; and von Braun and Grote 2000). Corruption may also increase with decentralization if personal or family ties begin to override legal or regulatory considerations (von Braun and Grote 2000). Government ownership can falter, leading to a reversal of the process, if decentralization results in stronger political opposition to the ruling party (Brosio 2002; Crook and Sverrisson 2001; von Braun and Grote 2000).

Although decentralization has a mixed record with regard to service delivery, there is general recognition that certain elements are necessary (but not sufficient) for positive impact. These include adequate financial resources, accountability for the use of resources, and government commitment and ownership (Crook and Sverrisson 2001; Manor 2003; OECD-DAC 2004; and Ahmad and others 2005). If decentralization takes place without these three conditions, diffused accountability and poor service delivery are likely to result. Some therefore argue that certain threshold levels of local capacity need to be in place to ensure that decentralized funds and services can be managed properly.

In short, the literature underscores that decentralization is not a panacea for poor service delivery. As the 2004 WDR notes: "If decentralization just replaces the functions of the central ministry with a slightly lower tier of government (a province or state), but everything else about the environment remains the same—compact, management, and client power—there is little reason to expect positive change." Thus, whether and how to decentralize or not is a question that can be answered only against the background of country-specific contexts and institutions.

This said, many countries decide to decentralize for political rather than economic reasons. Decentralization of power is seen as an instrument for absorbing regional and ethnic conflicts (von Braun and Grote 2000; Brosio 2002). Decentralization is also seen as encouraging civic participation because it allows communities to be consulted over matters that affect their daily lives (Katsiaouni 2003). The main issue before development practitioners in such cases is not whether to decentralize, because this political decision will often have been made and is outside the sphere of influence of technical specialists and policy advisers. Instead, it is how best to implement decentralization so that service delivery, particularly to the poor and disadvantaged, does not deteriorate.

Risks include macroeconomic instability, corruption, and elite capture.

Decentralization: Everyone Is Doing It

Most World Bank client countries have decentralized to at least one level of elected subnational government. Decentralization started as early as the 1960s in Nepal and Tanzania. These early efforts focused on social service delivery by local governments with participatory planning. By the 1980s many other countries were pursuing various forms of decentralization—in Latin America (Bolivia, Brazil, Chile, Colombia, Guatemala, Haiti, Jamaica, Nicaragua, and Mexico); Africa (Cameroon and Uganda); South Asia (Maldives, Nepal, and Sri Lanka); and East Asia (Vietnam). In the 1990s, many Eastern European countries began decentralizing, and by the late 1990s most countries served by the Bank were undergoing some form of devolution, delegation, or deconcentration of administrative, political, or fiscal authority and responsibility.

Certain elements are necessary (but not always sufficient) for a positive impact.

Countries have embraced decentralization for a range of reasons. In Eastern Europe and the former Soviet Union, decentralization was part of the political and economic transformation that came with the end of dominance by a highly centralized Soviet Union. In South Africa, Sri Lanka, and Indonesia, decentralization was also part of a strategy to dampen ethnic or regional discontent and conflict. In Chile, Uganda, and Côte d'Ivoire, decentralization was explicitly pursued to improve delivery of basic services (Shah 2004).

Most of the Bank's client countries have decentralized.

Each country has pursued its own form and pace of decentralization. Some countries have moved gradually, often stopping or reversing the process over the years or moving in "fits and starts." Experience in Albania, Peru, the Russian Federation, and Uganda fits this pattern. As indicated earlier, only a few countries have opted for a "Big Bang" approach. Among these is Ethiopia, which rapidly devolved substantial resources from central agencies to regions in 1993 (and only a few years later decentralized from regional to local levels), and the Philippines, which started in 1991 to devolve both political and expenditure responsibilities simultaneously to both regional and local governments and to transfer government staff from the center to these subnational governments.

Decentralization has differed between federal and unitary states. Although the latter can have different tiers of government among which responsibilities and powers are shared, in federal countries, such as Argentina, Brazil, Ethiopia, and Russia, the division of responsibilities and powers is typically enshrined in the Constitution and cannot be unilaterally revoked or altered by the central government. In unitary states, these responsibilities and powers are usually not based on a constitution, and the central government maintains the right to change the responsibilities and powers accorded to lower levels of government.

Some countries have decentralized gradually, often stopping or reversing the process.

Nevertheless, the distinction between federal and unitary states is blurred in some countries. Uganda, for example, is a unitary country; nevertheless, local governments and elected local councils are established through constitutional provisions and laws.

Overview of Bank Support for Decentralization

Lending volumes and trends

Bank support for decentralization has more often than not been embedded in multisector or sector loans, credits, and grants; few operations have been devoted solely to decentralization. As a result, establishing the total amounts and trends of Bank support for decentralization is very difficult (box 1.2).[2]

Using the Bank's coding system to identify projects in which decentralization is featured as

Box 1.2: Identifying World Bank Support for Decentralization Poses Challenges

The task team leader or a task team member assigns thematic codes to every Bank activity that directly serves the Bank's external clients. Every lending activity can be assigned up to 5 themes (selected from a list of 65), one of which is decentralization.

The code for decentralization falls under the auspices of the Public Sector Board and is defined broadly. For instance, it can accommodate any activity relating to "delivery of public services." The intent, of course, is that any such activity should involve decentralization in some form or fashion. The evaluation found cases where this would be difficult to argue. In addition, there are two other codes that are the responsibility of the Urban Sector Board and that cover decentralization-related activities: municipal governance and institution building and municipal finance.

The multiplicity of codes and the inevitable subjectivity in their assignment mean that the reliability of the system identifying Bank support for decentralization is not assured. Additionally, the system cannot report on how much of the total commitment may be attributed to support for decentralization, but can only point to loans or credits where decentralization or municipal finance is one element (as coded by the task team).

The evaluation reviewed the objectives of a large number of lending activities in the 20 countries where support for decentralization was assessed in depth. The goal was to understand whether they included support for decentralization as defined by the evaluation. Once these lending activities were narrowed down to 203 projects and programs, a more in-depth review of objectives and components allowed estimates to be made of the commitment for decentralization in each activity. About one-third of the total was found to be specifically targeted to decentralization-related support.

Source: IEG desk review.

a theme or activity, the Independent Evaluation Group (IEG) found that total commitments under these projects (spread over 89 client countries) over the period fiscal 1990–2006 amounted to $31.6 billion, 8 percent of total World Bank commitments during that period. For the most part, that lending was not uniquely or even primarily in support of decentralization, so it cannot be taken as a meaningful estimate of Bank financing for decentralization. This evaluation estimates that about one-third of this sum (about $10.6 billion) can be considered to have specifically targeted decentralization as defined for the purposes of this evaluation (see box 1.3). Note that this includes both still-open and closed commitments (the distinction is an important one).

Bank strategy

Decentralization is a cross-cutting theme, so no one network, sector board, or thematic group within the Bank has clear leadership, and no unifying decentralization strategy or guidelines have been articulated. Instead, since the late 1990s, several sector boards have issued relevant strategies. These strategies tend to treat decentralization as a cross-cutting issue with the potential to increase the efficiency of service delivery, but also with risks (box 1.3).

Bank approaches to decentralization

In the early 1980s, Bank support for decentralization was mainly in the urban sector,[3] starting in Latin America and spreading to other Regions.[4] In the late 1980s and early 1990s, the Bank focused on strengthening community participation in development planning and on increasing control over resources at the community level. In the mid-1990s, after several failed adjustment programs that led to deterioration in service delivery, the Bank began supporting delegation of the delivery of social services, in particular in education, health, and water, to local levels of government.

No single network, sector board, or thematic group oversees decentralization, and there is no overall Bank strategy in support of it.

Consequently, Bank support for fiscal decentralization and intergovernmental fiscal frameworks broadened. In the late 1990s, the emphasis shifted toward governance at intermediate government levels, focusing on fiscal reform, including strengthening of financial management, procurement, and related capacity. More

Box 1.3: Bank Strategies Reflect Multiple Perspectives on Decentralization

The Bank's approach to decentralization underwent a shift in the mid and late 1990s. It moved from neutral encouragement of stakeholder participation in decision making concerning resource allocation to more proactive support for bringing governments "closer" to the people.

The Bank's current approach is a more cautious one that emphasizes the need for strengthened institutions and risk mitigation. The 2000 Public Sector and Governance Strategy portrays decentralization as one of eight key elements of public sector reform. At the same time it recognizes the risks of elite capture and lack of capacity at the local level. The 2000 Urban and Local Government Strategy and the 2003 Rural Development Strategy also advocate a strong role for the Bank in strengthening local governments. The 2005 Social Development Strategy makes the case for linking community-driven development and decentralization.

In contrast, the 2007 health and 2005 education strategies recognize the trend toward decentralization in Bank client countries but are more cautious: they note the challenges and suggest a case-by-case approach to relying on or supporting local governments. For health, this reverses the approach of the 1997 strategy, which made decentralization one of three implementation pillars.

Finally, the 2003 Water Resources Sector Strategy, the 2003 Forestry Strategy, and the 2001 Environmental Strategy point out the risks of decentralization. The first suggests that optimum water resource management may need to be at the national or even international level, and the last two note that decentralization presents special challenges to natural resource management and environmental regulation and management (see appendix A for the relevant passages on decentralization in each of the sector strategies).

Source: World Bank data and IEG staff review.

Support started in the urban sector and spread to projects involving community participation, service delivery, and capacity building.

recently, with increasing devolution of responsibility for service delivery by several client countries, the Bank has further enlarged and deepened its support to include strengthening of local government institutions and capacity.

Throughout the review period, the Bank advocated and supported fiscal delegation and administrative deconcentration, although it encouraged some degree of central control and monitoring. Support for political decentralization covered a range of activities, including empowering local citizens to design and implement development activities, enhancing access to information on the use of public resources, and building the capacity of citizens to monitor service delivery.

Evaluation of Bank Support to Decentralization

As noted at the beginning of this chapter, the term "decentralization" means different things to different people. To bring in a sectoral perspective, the evaluation also reviewed operational activities for decentralization in the urban, education, health, and water sectors in countries in which Bank support was assessed in depth. The evaluation reviewed Bank support for decentralization in education in particular depth (see chapter 4), benefiting from case studies undertaken for a recent IEG evaluation of Bank support for education (IEG 2006a). This evaluation covers two key aspects of the Bank's support: its quality and its results. Appendix B details the evaluation methodology.

The evaluation addresses several questions regarding the quality of support. It reviews whether the support was based on a clear understanding of country context, whether it appropriately reflected the specific circumstances associated with decentralization in those countries, whether it was internally coherent and results based, and whether it was provided in collaboration with other development agencies.

The evaluation focuses on Bank support for strengthening decentralization frameworks and improving service delivery.

The evaluation focuses on intermediate outcomes rather than attempting to assess final outcomes for two reasons. One is paucity of data on final outcomes in Bank reports. The other is the challenge of attribution: even if data on service delivery and governance at the local government level were reliably available, it would be difficult to assess whether such improvements were due to decentralization, let alone to support for decentralization provided by the Bank, because of the many factors that influence such outcomes.

Figure 1.1 provides a framework to help trace how Bank input might help bring about final outcomes such as better service delivery and improved governance. As shown in the figure, three intermediate outcomes (results) are relevant: strengthened intergovernmental fiscal frameworks, enhanced administrative capacity, and increased accountability of subnational governments.

In addition, IEG divided the review of results along two lines: Bank support to strengthen decentralization frameworks and Bank support to improve service delivery. Bank instruments and design of the support, as well as the stated objectives of the lending, were often quite different between these two lines. Lending in support of frameworks was frequently provided through development policy loans (DPLs) or economic and sector work (ESW) and was aimed at public sector reform more broadly; lending for service delivery was more typically provided through investment and technical assistance projects and limited to sector-specific reform. For these reasons, this report discusses results separately, focusing first on the intermediate outcomes of Bank support for decentralization frameworks (chapter 3) and then on the intermediate outcomes of Bank support for service delivery in the education sector (chapter 4).

The discussion of intermediate results focuses only on those aspects that were supported by the Bank and does not assess the full results of decentralization. It is possible, for example, that decentralization has been working well overall in

Figure 1.1: Evaluation Framework for Assessing Results of Bank Support for Decentralization

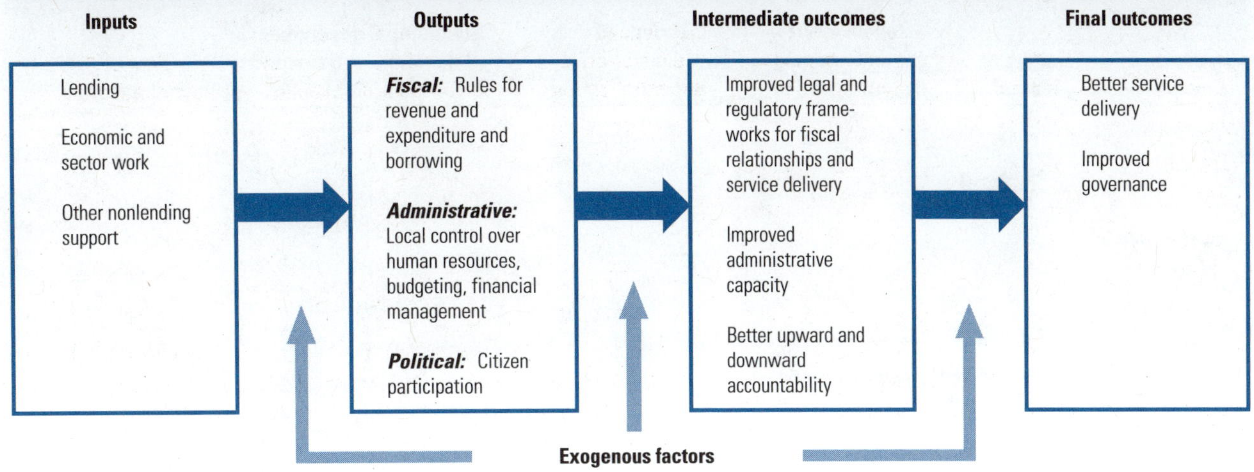

Source: IEG.

a country, even if the specific intermediate outcomes associated with Bank support have been less satisfactory, or vice versa. As with all IEG evaluations, the findings on the results of Bank support therefore cannot be generalized to a country's overall effort.

To capture Bank support in different country contexts, IEG selected 20 countries from the set of 89 that were coded as receiving Bank support for decentralization, municipal governance and institutional strengthening, or municipal finance. Given that decentralization is a process that takes significant time to achieve maturity, the evaluation reviewed Bank support for decentralization to these 20 countries between fiscal 1990 and 2007. The set of countries reviewed for the evaluation includes countries representing all Regions, with both small and large populations, and exhibiting eligibility for both International Bank for Reconstruction and Development and International Development Association funding, federal and unitary systems, Big Bang and gradual approaches, as well as past or present conflict-affected status (see table 1.1 for a typology of the 20 countries).

The commitments of financial support to these 20 countries represented 47 percent of the Bank's total commitment to the 89 countries that contained some sort of World Bank support for decentralization.

Figure 1.2 shows the annual commitments of World Bank financial support related to decentralization in the 20 countries, with a cumulative total of about $10.2 billion. The majority of these projects are now closed, but figure 1.2 also includes still-active commitments. To assess the quality and results of Bank support, the evaluation considered only 203 lending activities that closed before June 30, 2007 (about 30 percent of which were DPLs, the remainder being investment projects). The commitments associated with the parts of these activities that related specifically to decentralization total $7.4 billion. In addition to the closed activities, a few open activities were reviewed to see if there were any discernable shifts in the quality of Bank support for decentralization.

Chapter 2 contains the evaluation's findings on the quality of Bank support for decentralization to the 20 countries. To assess quality, all relevant documents, including Country Assistance Strategies (CASs), ESW, and lending documents (appraisal through implementation completion for the 203 closed projects) were examined. A three-point scale

The evaluation assessed Bank support to 20 countries that received about half of all Bank funding with decentralization-related activities.

Table 1.1: Typology of Countries Where Bank Support for Decentralization Was Reviewed in Depth

Country	Unitary or federal	Recent effort at strengthening decentralization	Type of administrative decentralization	Subnational government dependent on transfers for >75% of revenue	Type of decentralization
Albania	U	2000	Devolution	Y	Gradual
Bolivia	U	1994	Deconcentration	Y	Gradual
Brazil	F	1988	Devolution	N	Gradual
Burkina Faso	U	1998	Deconcentration	Y	Gradual
Ethiopia	F	1993	Devolution	N	Big Bang
India	F	1993	Deconcentration	Y	Gradual
Indonesia	U	2000	Devolution	Y	Big Bang
Madagascar	U	2003	Deconcentration	Y	Gradual
Morocco	U	1992	Deconcentration	N	Gradual
Nepal	U	1999	Deconcentration	Y	Gradual
Nicaragua	U	1988	Deconcentration	Y	Gradual
Pakistan	F	2001	Devolution	Y	Big Bang
Peru	U	2003	Deconcentration	Y	Gradual
Philippines	U	1991	Devolution	N	Big Bang
Russia	F	1999	Devolution	N	Gradual
Rwanda	U	2000	Deconcentration	Y	Gradual
Sierra Leone	U	2004	Deconcentration	Y	Gradual
Tanzania	U	1997	Deconcentration	Y	Gradual
Uganda	U	1993	Devolution	Y	Gradual
Yemen, Rep. of	U	2000	Deconcentration	Y	Gradual

Source: IEG desk review.
Note: All local governments established through elections. F = federal; U = unitary.

(high, medium, and low) was used to rate the quality of Bank support.

For decentralization frameworks (chapter 3), results were assessed in the 20 countries listed in table 1.1. A four-point scale (high, substantial, modest, and negligible) was used to rate the results of Bank support, and a before-and-after methodology was used to assess progress at the country level.

The evaluation assessed whether Bank support helped improve decentralization frameworks in 20 countries and service delivery in education in 6.

For service delivery (chapter 4), IEG assessed Bank support for education services in a subset of six countries. These were selected based on the amount of support provided by the Bank and the availability of evaluative information from other IEG reports. Given the small size of the sample, the assessment is aimed only at providing some insights into the issues, strengths, and weaknesses that have characterized at least some Bank work on decentralization related to service delivery.

To assess the results of Bank support at the country level in addition to reviews of Implementation and Completion and Results Reports (ICRs) and other Bank self-assessments, IEG undertook field missions to 8 of the 20 countries—Burkina Faso, India, Madagascar, Peru, the Philippines, Russia, Tanzania, and Uganda—to gather additional evidence regarding the decentralization efforts. Additionally, IEG's Country Assistance Evaluation (CAE) mission to Indonesia and other recent CAEs on Albania and the Republic of Yemen provided in-

Figure 1.2: Bank Support for Decentralization to 20 Countries, Fiscal 1990–2007 (includes still-open activities between 2000 and 2007)

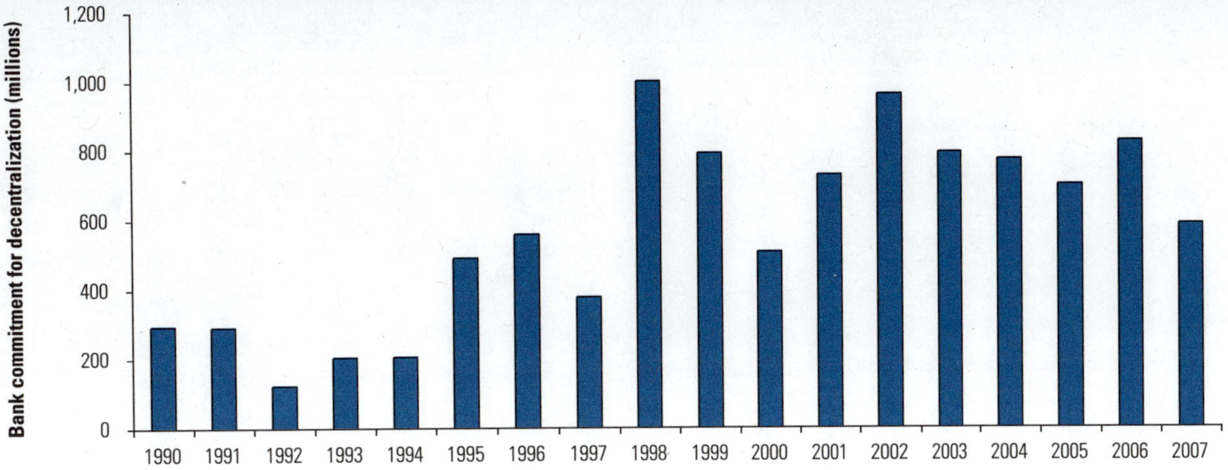

Source: World Bank database.

Note: This includes total commitment of $10.22 billion specifically targeted at decentralization activities (that is, all projects with a decentralization, municipal governance, or municipal finance theme).

depth information on decentralization issues. Several IEG Project Performance Assessments Reports also deepened the understanding of results.

IEG participated in a workshop on decentralization organized by the Organisation for Economic Co-operation and Development–Development Assistance Committee (OECD-DAC) Informal Working Group on Decentralization and Local Governance in September 2007 and issued a joint survey on donor collaboration to the participants. The results of that survey are integrated into this report. With financial support from the Norwegian Agency for International Development (better known as Norad), two participatory field assessments in the Philippines and Uganda were undertaken to bring the voices of client country citizens into the evaluation in a systematic way. Other stakeholders consulted during missions are listed in online appendix D (see http://worldbank.org/ieg/decentralization/download.html).

Chapter 2

Evaluation Essentials

- The quality of Bank support for decentralization has improved significantly in the past five years.
- In countries that have devolved responsibilities for some service delivery, Bank support for local governments is more recent and in most cases began only after devolution was well under way.
- Analytical work is mostly sectoral and is typically not used outside the relevant sector.
- Treatment of political economy issues in ESW is typically weak and—even where it exists—rarely influences recommendations.
- Donor collaboration on decentralization is increasing, although several challenges remain; harmonization of financial management and procurement processes must be catalyzed to reduce the costs to local governments of doing business with the Bank.

Senegalese village center. Photo by Curt Carnemark, courtesy of the World Bank Photo Library.

The Quality of Bank Support

This chapter details the results of IEG's assessment of the quality of Bank support, both analytical/advisory and financial, in the 20 countries over the evaluation period. The assessment reviewed Bank support to understand whether it was based on a clear understanding of country context, whether the support appropriately reflected the circumstances in these countries and the Bank's own diagnoses of decentralization issues, whether the support was internally coherent and results based, and whether the support was provided in collaboration with other development partners.

The assessment is based on a desk review of all Bank country strategies, relevant ESW on decentralization, and all World Bank financing (projects and fast-disbursing loans) in support of client countries' public sector as well as of the urban, health, and education sectors. In the eight countries where field missions were conducted, the findings of the desk review were validated through interviews with relevant client country stakeholders as well as bilateral and multilateral development agency representatives.

The quality of Bank support for decentralization during the entire evaluation period was of medium quality, but there was significant improvement in the last five years of the evaluation period, when the quality of Bank work was high in about two-thirds of the 20 countries. Still, better coordinated and more comprehensive approaches are needed in about one-third of the sample countries where the quality challenge endures.

The Quality of Bank Analytical Work on Decentralization

IEG found decentralization-related diagnostic reports for 16 of the 20 sample countries (see online appendix E).[1] Of the remaining four countries, analytical work is ongoing in three. In a few countries, including Uganda and Sierra Leone, even though there was no analytical work prior to Bank financing, the operational work was undertaken in collaboration with other development partners, based on successful United Nations Capital Development Fund (UNCDF) pilot projects.[2]

In about half of the sample countries, the Bank undertook analytical work within five years of a decentralization law being passed. In the other half, the Bank neither anticipated nor examined the implications of the decentralization law for key areas of the Bank's work within the five-year period (see table 2.1). In Pakistan, timely and extensive ESW, some of which was undertaken

Table 2.1: Timeliness of ESW in 20 Sample Countries

ESW undertaken	Percent of cases
Within two years after decentralization law was passed	20
2–5 years after decentralization law was passed	35
5–10 years after decentralization law was passed	20
No completed ESW found that dealt substantially with decentralization	25

Source: World Bank data.

jointly with other major development partners, influenced financial support from the Bank for decentralization in the country. In Brazil, an in-depth study of the challenges of decentralization to the municipal level fed into the design of Bank support for municipalities.

During the 1990s, analytical work was mostly sectoral in nature, and the type of work done often depended on which unit did it.

During the 1990s, the concentration of analytical work was on sector-specific aspects of decentralization, depending on the Bank unit that undertook the analysis. Such analyses influenced subsequent Bank interventions in the sector in question. Beyond this, the analyses had very limited influence in that they did not lead to a holistic understanding of decentralization and its implications or of cross-sectoral synergies. As a result, they were unable to catalyze the formulation of coherent country-level decentralization support strategies, even under circumstances where the client countries had devolved service delivery to local governments across multiple sectors.

In Peru and Russia, the analyses initially concentrated on the fiscal aspects of decentralization and paid less attention to the close linkages with many aspects of broader public sector reform. In some countries, such as Nepal and Sierra Leone, the Bank studied the implications of decentralization through the lens of Public Expenditure Reviews, which tended in some cases to highlight expenditure issues without linking them to revenue-side issues, notably the resources needed to implement devolved spending responsibilities.

Sector analyses in health and education frequently had at least some treatment of the implications of decentralization, but the sector perspective meant that major cross-cutting issues of local government accountability and capacity were not addressed (for instance, in Brazil, Burkina Faso, Ethiopia, and the Philippines). In India and Morocco, a rural-urban segmentation of the analysis was predominant, resulting in the (sometimes virtually simultaneous) preparation of separate reports focusing on rural and urban local governments, respectively.

Until recently, the treatment of political economy issues in most ESW was weak. Most pieces did not discuss the roles of important interest groups and different public officials. Insofar as political economy factors were discussed, they tended to be portrayed as post hoc explanations for past government policy failures. Most of the earlier ESW did not anticipate the responses of important interest groups (such as teachers and public sector unions) or of public sector officials to proposed institutional reforms.

Although the Bolivia Institutional and Governance Review (World Bank 2006b) and the Madagascar study on decentralization (World Bank 2004c) stand out for their treatment of political economy issues, the Tanzania study on fiscal decentralization (World Bank 2006k) and the study on Pakistan's reform of provincial finances in the context of devolution (World Bank 2000b) offer only limited treatment of such issues. Additionally, in fewer than half of the 16 countries for which decentralization-related diagnostic reports could be found, the ESW examined the fiscal costs of decentralization for the various levels of government. As a result, recommendations were often prefaced with general headings and discussions of "interna-

Box 2.1: Good Practice ESW in Bolivia

The Bolivia Institutional and Governance Review *Towards an Inclusive Decentralization* (World Bank 2006b) is a good-practice ESW that provides guidance for Bank interventions in support of specific sectors in the country as well as for the design of a CAS. Its strong features include the following:

1. It takes a comprehensive view of the decentralization process in Bolivia. It pays careful attention to potential problems of fiscal discipline—identifying them as most crucial—but also relates these to service delivery in key sectors, to broader governance issues, and to accountability, all within a common framework focusing on institutions and incentives.
2. It establishes trade-offs across goals. In contrast with the limitations of a sector-specific report, the comprehensiveness of this review forces the authors to consider whether multiple reform goals might be mutually incompatible. For example, the review discusses the trade-offs between efficiency and equity, especially in relation to the difficulties of enhancing local revenue mobilization and otherwise strengthening incentives that local officials face in contexts marked by dramatic inter-regional and urban-rural income inequities. It buttresses the discussion with detailed data and analysis relating to such inequities and highlights trade-offs when discussing reform possibilities.
3. It recommends the most attractive ways of avoiding, or at least minimizing, risks associated with an ineffectively designed and politically motivated decentralization program. It recommends a sequence of reforms and emphasizes trade-offs associated with each possible choice.
4. The review concludes that decentralization to regional governments in Bolivia is likely to be successful in improving either service delivery or local governance under existing conditions. It sets out why the Institutional and Governance Review arrives at this assessment and relates it to the recent history of municipal decentralization and political economy in Bolivia, as well as outcomes in other countries that faced similar circumstances.

Source: World Bank documents.

tional best practice." They were disconnected from the circumstances of the countries.

Only in four countries (accounting for some 10 percent of reports reviewed) did ESW meaningfully review and assess Bank support for decentralization and provide recommendations on suitable entry points, phasing of decentralization-related reforms, and necessary preconditions for Bank support. In the remaining countries, an opportunity was missed for ESW to deepen its influence on the design of Bank support.

The Madagascar ESW (World Bank 2004c) is notable in that it identified conditions under which the decentralization of certain activities might be desirable and proceeded to compare these conditions systematically with the actual situation. This led to a set of phased recommendations, some of which involved centralization. The Tanzania report on fiscal decentralization (World Bank 2006k) is good practice in terms of the clarity with which it provides recommendations for the design of Bank support for decentralization.

Although up to a point all ESW discusses monitoring systems, this was done meaningfully in only seven countries, where the ESW assessed the quality of existing systems, areas of weaknesses, and the nature of data that needed to be collected. The Madagascar ESW is good practice in this area and recommended that a monitoring system be established as a first-phase activity before deepening decentralization.

Discussion of political economy in most ESW has been weak.

More recently, decentralization has received more comprehensive treatment in 40 percent of the countries (Madagascar 2004; Pakistan 2004; Bolivia 2006; Russia 2005; East Asia and the Pacific 2006, covering Indonesia and the Philippines; Burkina Faso 2007; and Ethiopia 2007). The associated reports seek to understand the important shift in governance that decentralization has brought about and the implications for the development agenda, including Bank strategies. Although the reports address the issues from different angles (for example, fiscal reform in Russia

Only in four countries did ESW provide guidance to Bank staff on preconditions or entry points for Bank support.

versus service delivery in Ethiopia), the analysis of decentralization is more comprehensive than in the past, with a focus on both the demand and supply side aspects of decentralization and their complex interaction.

The majority of these reports were prepared by multisectoral teams in collaboration with other development partners and with the participation of country stakeholders. This has enhanced the quality of the analysis and ownership by the stakeholders. In Russia, for example, stakeholders interviewed for this evaluation noted the participatory manner in which the analysis of decentralization was undertaken and were particularly appreciative of the technical knowledge that Bank teams brought to bear in helping them design their local systems. (Examples in box 2.2 on page 21 illustrate the importance of sound analysis of country context for the design of Bank support.)

The influence of broader Bank analyses of decentralization is unclear.

The Bank has also prepared broader analyses of decentralization issues. The public face of this work was the decentralization page of the Poverty Reduction and Economic Management (PREM) Public Sector Web site. In addition, "Rethinking Decentralization in Developing Countries" (World Bank 1998b), issued by the PREM anchor, provided guidance on moving away from a normative approach to decentralization. The "Decentralization Briefing Notes" (Litvack and Seddon 1999), published by the World Bank Institute in collaboration with PREM, contained 21 brief, well-focused papers on aspects of the rationale for decentralization, project design, service delivery, and potential impacts of decentralization. *Fiscal Decentralization and the Challenges of Hard Budget Constraints* (Rodden and Eskeland 2003), a set of studies to guide Bank staff and other practitioners, provided guidance on how to avoid excessive debt accumulation as subnational units gained greater fiscal independence and worked through the implications for how to decentralize (or not).

A final work, "Decentralization and Governance" (World Bank 2001a), guided staff on avoiding local capture and improving local governments' responsiveness to their citizens. There is little evidence that this set of publications had substantial influence within the Bank, although this evaluation found that other development partners were aware of them and considered the Bank as having significant technical knowledge and expertise in this area.

Coherence of Lending with Country Priorities and Bank Analysis

The evaluation assessed the extent to which each Bank lending operation was prepared jointly with the relevant client country, reflected country-specific circumstances, and was rooted in the Bank's own diagnosis of the decentralization process in the country.

Participation of country stakeholders

Country stakeholder participation in the preparation of Bank lending was high or substantial in 14 of the 20 countries. Stakeholder participation was highest in the Africa Region and lowest in the Middle East and North Africa Region. Stakeholder participation was also high in Russia, where government and other stakeholders reported that they had led the project design, with the Bank bringing its technical knowledge, including a comparative perspective on good practices across countries, to bear.

Reflection of country-specific circumstances

Weaknesses in the understanding and treatment of political economy risks in ESW and in project design have given rise to overly ambitious objectives in Bank lending. Bank lending documents typically acknowledge and address these risks. However, they also tend to assume that the Bank can mitigate virtually any relevant risk. Even serious risks (high-probability and/or high-loss events) are considered to be contained by various mitigation measures.

In Peru, a better dissemination strategy was expected to address risks associated with the lack of consensus on decentralization. In Pakistan, the threat of rapid disengagement by the Bank was expected to mitigate the risk of dwindling political will to carry out reforms. The relative downplaying of risks in this manner makes "stretch" objectives appear more credible and realistic.

In contrast, overly ambitious objectives entail lower achievements—hence reduced effectiveness—vis-à-vis the former. Additionally, in many cases, sector-level activities did not display awareness of ongoing general fiscal reforms. The Tanzania Human Resource Development Project (approved in 1997) focused on facility-based decentralization, transparent fiscal transfers on a per capita basis, and community participation; this marginalized the role of subnational governments that a 1997 law on decentralization provided for.[3]

Influence of own diagnosis in design of Bank support

In 12 of the 16 countries for which ESW was carried out, at least one report appears to have influenced the design of one or more Bank lending operations. Most of these operations were DPLs with specific reform measures ("conditions") derived from decentralization-related studies (Albania, Brazil, Burkina Faso, and Pakistan). The influence of ESW on the design of investment projects was not as clear.

The Tanzania decentralization study (2001e) provided the Bank with a basis for supporting the local government program during a phase when there was not yet a consensus among development partners about whether and how to support decentralization. The municipal sector decentralization study in Brazil (1992a) contributed significantly to paving the way for municipal development loans in many states.

Two reports on Russia (one on the fiscal costs of reform and the other on regional-local reform) contributed to the government's fiscal decentralization reform plan for the medium term at the regional and municipal levels (World Bank 2005h, 2005i); they also supported the design of the Bank's Fiscal Federalism and Regional Fiscal Reform Loan. Regarding the remaining four countries for which ESW was carried out—Ethiopia, Morocco, Nicaragua, and the Philippines—either the influence of ESW on Bank support is not evident or the ESW is too recent to assess whether it has had meaningful influence.

Weak understanding of political economy issues led to overly ambitious objectives.

Analytical work prepared by one unit generally had little influence on operations prepared by other units. For example, an analysis of fiscal decentralization and intergovernmental finances in Albania (World Bank 1994a) pointed to the lack of clarity in allocating responsibilities among the different levels of government in the social sectors. It cautioned that Bank support for decentralization must first address this lack of clarity and investigate the benefits of decentralizing noninfrastructure services in the social sectors. However, the 1998 Albania Health System Recovery and Development Project supported the decentralization of health services to the Tirana Regional Health Authority, thereby in effect adding a layer of management costs without ensuring the autonomy necessary to realize the benefits. This aspect of the project has complicated decentralization in the health sector and now calls for corrective action.[4]

ESW frequently pointed to measures subsequently supported by DPLs.

Differing sectoral or thematic perspectives can give rise to inconsistencies (and ultimately to reduced development effectiveness) in a Bank country program. In the Philippines, PREM studies (World Bank 1999b, 2004g) identified a need to operationalize the 1996 framework for Local Government Unit (LGU) financing, including transforming the Municipal Development Fund (MDF) into a full-fledged financial intermediary and requiring government financial intermediaries (GFIs) to help LGUs reduce their reliance on government transfers.[5] The PREM studies note that access to private sources of capital remains largely untapped because of the virtual monopoly of GFIs and the MDF.[6]

Operations have tended not to consider relevant analysis done by other units.

In contrast, a 2006 project by a regional urban unit continues to support lending by GFIs to local governments because, according to the project documents, private sector funding for local government infrastructure is still limited, and increasing it can only be a long-term objective. A proposed urban sector project aims to strengthen the MDF (still nestled in the Department of Finance) to support the lower tier of LGUs.[7]

Inconsistencies in objectives across individual sector interventions reduced development effectiveness at a country level.

In Morocco, a PREM report (World Bank 1992b) noted that the key issue with municipal governments was not lack of funding, but lack of capacity. Yet the 1993 first MDF project provided funding for infrastructure loans to municipalities after dropping a significant capacity-building component because of (central) government reluctance to use loan proceeds for the latter purpose. The second loan, in 1998, which continued lending to municipalities, was also approved without any provision for capacity building because of resistance from the government to borrow for capacity building.

Although each of the individual sector or thematic perspectives within a given Bank country program may be underpinned by a sound rationale, improved development effectiveness requires that tensions between differing perspectives be resolved, ideally through a country-owned strategy or at least through a unifying framework for Bank assistance.

Internal Consistency and Results Orientation

Internal consistency

Much of the Bank's support for decentralization appears to have seized opportunities as they arose across sectors. However, the multiplicity of units that support decentralization, the differences in approach across the various units, and the diversity of objectives underlying Bank support for decentralization have entailed uncoordinated support at the expense of development effectiveness. Because responsibility for decentralization-related support to operational units is split among PREM, Social Development, Urban Development, and other sectoral units, the support is often fragmented in a field where a highly collaborative and coordinated approach is essential for effectiveness. As a result, support to client countries has not capitalized on the significant depth and breadth of expertise on the subject that exists within the Bank.[8]

Inconsistencies arose between centralization of tax authority and decentralization of expenditures, as well as in human resources treatment.

One illustration of this is Nicaragua, where a sector-level perspective encouraged the adoption of a law that introduced a transparent system of formula-based transfers to municipalities. These transfers effectively contributed to the equalization process and addressed an existing unfunded mandate on municipalities' part. However, they also raised new issues of macroeconomic-level fiscal imbalance, particularly because municipalities did not have commensurate expenditure responsibilities. The transfers contributed mainly to increased employment and salaries at the municipal level rather than investment in local priorities.[9]

The Bank has since begun helping revise this result through DPLs, where corrective measures feature among the reforms supported by these operations.[10] As a Bank Policy Note (World Bank 2004e) rightly concludes, "Without an appropriate institutional framework and monitoring system, hasty and aggressive decentralization can lead to waste of resources, a worsening of the provision of public services, and increased macroeconomic instability."[11]

Differences in ways of pursuing macroeconomic stability and equity have given rise to some inconsistencies across objectives in at least 6 of the 20 countries. For example, recentralizing the tax base can advance both equity and macroeconomic stability and reduce fiscal imbalances; however, recentralization also reduces the fiscal autonomy of subnational units, thereby reducing their ability to respond to local needs and priorities.

In Tanzania, PREM staff, together with the International Monetary Fund (IMF), supported the centralization of local revenue-raising authority, and the urban unit supported the decentralization of expenditures. In Russia, revenue administration has been recentralized with Bank support, ostensibly to ensure macroeconomic stability and equitable allocation of revenue at the regional level. However, this has negatively affected the revenue autonomy of several regional governments. In four countries, tax administration projects were implemented after the passage of a decentralization law, but the projects dealt primarily with centralized revenue administration structures.

If well designed and well executed, administrative decentralization should involve the rationalization and reallocation of human resources and result in the enhanced efficiency of government services. The evaluation found that in a few countries, including Bolivia, Pakistan, and Tanzania, macroeconomic adjustment programs required the central government to contain the wage bill. At the same time, subnational governments were under pressure to hire more staff to meet their newly assigned responsibilities. Not surprisingly, neither wage containment nor efficient human resource capacity build-up were achieved under such circumstances.

Differing approaches to decentralization have led to tensions in several countries where Bank support was not coordinated across the units delivering the support. In the majority of the country cases reviewed, a community-driven development (CDD) approach, as typically featured in Bank support (essentially a form of deconcentration that transfers implementation responsibility to community groups), generated some tensions. This happened in some situations where responsibilities for service delivery and community participation had been devolved or delegated by law, often to newly created local governments.

Box 2.2: An Incomplete Understanding Reduces Effectiveness of Support

The **Ethiopia Health and Education Sector** projects (each $100 million, approved in 1999) were designed after a social sector review that did not fully consider decentralization issues and before a 2000 study of regionalization that undertook a more in-depth review of the issues. Deficient project design and weak institutional capacity partly explain the weak outcome ratings.

In **Nicaragua**, without prior analysis of the institutional framework for decentralization, Bank support encouraged the government to require a transfer of resources to municipalities in the (not entirely correct) belief that the latter were subjected to unfunded mandates. Now the challenge for Bank support to the Nicaraguan authorities is to help bring about a transfer of expenditure responsibilities to match a predetermined level of resource transfers.

In **Bolivia**, without comprehensive prior ESW, both the first and second Programmatic Structural Adjustment Credits (PSACs) (which incorporated 39 reform measures, 27 of them relating directly to decentralization) failed to achieve their objectives, owing in part to ongoing conflict and in part to an incomplete understanding of the highly complex institutional setting. The Ministry of Finance, the counterpart for the PSAC, is today an additional body setting decentralization policies, along with two other national coordinating bodies for decentralization, complicating the institutional framework for decentralization (see World Bank 2004b, pp. 16 and 20).

In **the Republic of Yemen**, without prior ESW, the 2002 country strategy planned to provide support for ambitious decentralization objectives under the assumption that a broad consensus had been achieved around the decentralization agenda through the 2000 Local Government Law. Some analytical work initiated in 2002 was delivered in 2005 but not published because of disagreements with the government. A Learning and Innovation Loan to support decentralization was appraised, but not carried through to approval, again because of a disagreement with the country authorities on the approach. The subsequent CAS candidly noted that government commitment to decentralization was questionable. Meanwhile, the United Nations Capital Development Fund (UNCDF) and other development partners in the Republic of Yemen have ongoing decentralization-related activities in the country and believe that the Bank-advocated social fund approach is undermining the effectiveness of local governments.

Source: Desk review of Bank documents.

CDD can strengthen voices of local communities but if not carefully designed can undermine the role of local governments.

Although CDD can strengthen the capacity of local governments to participate in development activities, enhance community voice in local development, and reduce risks of political capture, it also relies in many cases on centralized allocation of resources[12] and/or parallel community bodies for implementation (see box 2.3). This can undermine the local government's role in development activities. That said, increasingly, the approach to resource allocation and coordination with local governments in Bank-supported activities may be changing.

Similar tensions have arisen where Bank support was not fully aligned with the client country's decentralization strategy and policies. In India, although Bank support for fiscal discipline and reform at the state level helped strengthen macroeconomic stability, its support in the social and rural sectors was not equally consistent with the country's policies for deepening decentralization. During the evaluation period, the Bank supported centrally planned and designed social programs and often created parallel community-level institutions to oversee and monitor services that were distinct from the village local government or panchayat in charge of local development and community participation.[13]

In the Philippines, after the ambitious decentralization program of 1991, health services were placed entirely under the authority of local governments, but the Bank supported centrally planned and designed health sector interventions through project implementation units. This is not a problem per se; in some industrialized countries, deconcentrated mechanisms have led to effective service delivery. Furthermore, in many situations (for example, a concerted effort to meet the Millennium Development Goals), such a centralized approach may be necessary if local governments do not have the capacity or the political will to allocate funding. However, such a deconcentrated approach to implementation can reduce the roles of local governments to whom delivery of service has been devolved or delegated.

Recent efforts have attempted to mitigate such tensions. In the Philippines, the Kalahi CIDSS project (2003) has supported more coordinated ways of working with local institutions. In this project, allocation of resources is undertaken in a competitive manner by village-level government units in participating municipalities. In Tanzania, the second social action fund attempted to provide expanded, more explicit roles for district and village governments. These efforts notwithstanding, development partners continue to perceive the fund as an opaque instrument, largely because of the centralization of allocation decisions with the final oversight and responsibility resting in a project implementation unit in the president's office. Partners argue that this weakens the role of local governments in a process of devolution. The Bank's 2005 Social Development Strategy (see appendix A), which calls for greater linkages between decentralization and CDD, is likely to encourage greater coordination with local governments under CDD initiatives.[14]

Box 2.3: CDD and Local Governments in the Philippines

Interviews with local stakeholders of the Bank-supported Water Districts Development Project demonstrate the tensions between approaches that primarily involve community groups as implementers of local development activities and those that involve local governments. The *Barangay* (village government) officials commented that it was difficult to accept the "Bank condition" that the water and sanitation services should be managed by a community association and not by the *Barangay*, because they felt that they have the mandate to provide these services under the Decentralization Code. The *Barangay* captain in Mabunao noted that the city and the *Barangay* had agreed in principle that after the project closed, the facility should be turned over to the *Barangay*. At the same time, the community association officers said that the project increased citizen participation, accountability, and transparency. They felt that although the community had previously depended only on the *Barangay* and municipal governments to provide water and sanitation services, the citizens were now more empowered as co-owners of the facility, with a voice in management.

Source: IEG field assessment of the Water Districts Development Project in the Philippines.

Results orientation of Bank support

During the evaluation period, Bank operations have focused monitoring on fiscal decentralization. They have tracked indicators such as transfers to subnational governments or increases in own-source revenue. However, IEG found that in 10 of the 20 country cases, the most recent country strategies had broadened their focus to include assessments of the performance of local governments and institutions.

At an operational level, about 43 percent of Bank decentralization-related lending activities in 11 countries during the evaluation period include at least one indicator to measure the results of decentralization (with some activities in Sierra Leone, Russia, and Uganda representing good practices). In the remaining nine countries, such monitoring indicators were not found. In the 11 countries, the indicators have been tracked in more than three-fourths of ICRs, although several reports discuss achievements in a qualitative manner. Intermediate outcome indicators are rare, and even when available they are vague, such as "number of well-functioning municipal councils." Neither appraisal documents nor ICRs define "well functioning."

A review of still-active projects shows that the improvement in recent CASs is reflected at the operational level. Newer operations include fiscal and administrative indicators such as the share of unconditional transfers and own-source revenue in local government budgets, the number of municipalities with development plans prepared in accordance with guidelines, and local staffing levels. Accountability indicators are also included, to track trends in voice and participation (number of local authorities who hold regular community meetings with published minutes, public access to relevant information) and to track local government accountability (comparison of unit costs of infrastructure built by local governments with those of line agencies, transparent financial management systems at the local levels). Most operations also set aside funds for household and beneficiary surveys to assess citizen perceptions of service delivery.

Ensuring that these monitoring mechanisms are properly maintained and systematically reported on during project implementation will be the key to enhancing knowledge on the links between decentralization and improved service delivery.

Inconsistencies can arise when Bank support is not aligned with country strategies.

The recently introduced Public Financial Management (PFM) Performance Measurement Framework[15] contains two indicators (transparency of intergovernmental fiscal relations and public availability of information on resource allocations received by service delivery units) that can help monitor aspects of decentralized service delivery at a country level. These indicators will underpin an assessment of progress.

This framework has also been adapted by development partners in preparing local government fiduciary assessments such as in Tanzania (World Bank 2006l). This is a good practice report led by the government of Tanzania. It provides a candid assessment of fiduciary issues at the local level as well as quantitative information on local government performance. The Bank has also helped develop a checklist for assessing the distributional impact of decentralization as part of an effort to improve poverty and social impact analysis of decentralization (Kaiser 2006). Strengthening and replicating such efforts can lead to improved monitoring and evaluation (M&E) of local government performance.

Supporting client countries to monitor the progress and impact of decentralization at the project level is important.

Collaboration among Development Partners

Collaboration with development partners is increasing at the country level. A review of recent country strategies indicates that 55 percent included high or substantial collaboration among development partners. The strategies included a joint strategy for decentralization as well as joint diagnostic and analytical work and lending activities within a context of general alignment and harmonization at the country level. At the operational

Active projects show improved attention to monitoring fiscal, administrative, voice, and accountability dimensions of decentralization.

Collaboration with development partners has included joint strategy development, analytical work, and lending.

level, about two-thirds of all activities have been prepared with high or substantial donor collaboration.

Mechanisms for collaboration on decentralization support are increasing and include both formal and informal working groups. In the Philippines, the Bank has been instrumental in initiating the Philippines Development Forum, a government mechanism for facilitating substantive dialogue on the country's development agenda. It has also helped facilitate a working group devoted to decentralization and local governments, which has reportedly given local governments a voice through their associations.

Collaboration with development partners in decentralization has increased in the majority of the evaluation countries.

In several countries, including Tanzania and Uganda, significant diagnostic work is now undertaken jointly with the development of the Public Expenditure and Financial Accountability (PEFA) PFM checklist and the OECD-DAC tool for assessment of national procurement systems. These tools have been adapted to cover local levels and are applied jointly by the government's key development partners.[16] Joint assistance strategies in several of the 20 cases are helping establish a strategic framework for assistance, leading to joint missions and assessments, and supporting clients with the development of common measurement indicators. However, it is clear from donor responses to a questionnaire and other reviews by donor groups that development partners need to deepen collaboration on support for decentralization (box 2.4).[17]

Collaboration among development partners is improving, but harmonization is progressing slowly.

This evaluation also finds that harmonization of development partners' financial management requirements and procurement practices at the local level has generally been slow in the 20 countries. Nevertheless, there are noteworthy examples of progress. In the Philippines, major development partners harmonized their procurement guidelines and financial reporting requirements with the central government. This has helped harmonization at the subnational levels also. In Brazil, an agreement has been reached among the Inter-American Development Bank (IADB), the World Bank, and the government on the use of country systems for financial reporting. Implementation of this agreement still lies ahead.

Although Bank instruments such as Sector-wide Approaches have sought to harmonize financial reporting and procurement procedures at various sector levels, these efforts do not necessarily lead to improved harmonization at the local levels. In Tanzania, each local government continues to have multiple bank accounts for each sector project or program, and sometimes separate ones within each sector to accommodate the reporting obligations of the various development partners. The shift to greater use of country systems could help reduce such transaction costs for Bank client countries.

Overall, the evaluation finds that the quality of Bank support for decentralization was of medium (neither high nor low) quality during the evaluation period but has improved significantly since the early 2000s; recent quality has been high in two-thirds of the 20 countries.

Recent Bank analytical work is leading to a better understanding of the broad implications of decentralization for service delivery and governance and is in turn influencing the design of country strategies as a whole. At an operational level, support for greater clarity in decentralization policies is typically combined with technical assistance to strengthen the capacity and accountability of different government levels (and the linkages between them). Finally, the Bank is getting better at ensuring substantial client participation and ownership among the different levels of government and among citizens in the design of assistance and support to monitor the results of decentralization. Collaboration with other development partners is improving but is still not consistently effective.

Box 2.4: Development Partner Views on World Bank Decentralization Performance

Seven development partners responded to IEG's questionnaire on coordination (see below). Most appreciated the substantial technical competence and experience of Bank staff and their presence in countries. They also appreciated the influence of the Bank's financial resources on national policies and its ability to get the country government to focus on critical issues.

However, respondents noted that the Bank was often unwilling to work with other bilateral partners and that it sometimes funded conflicting programs and developed parallel systems. They also remarked on the tendency of the Bank and other multilateral agencies, particularly in Asia, to segregate Regions or sectors. They also opined that Bank staff are "politically naïve" and do not have a historical perspective essential in this area.

Question	High–substantial (%)	Modest–negligible (%)
Extent of your agency's collaboration with Bank in supporting decentralization	29	71
Extent of your agency's collaboration with other partners	71	29
Extent to which Bank approach is consistent with that of your agency	100	
Extent of satisfaction with Bank approach to decentralization	33	66

Source: Responses from seven partner agencies to IEG questionnaire (2007).

The lack of a unifying strategy or framework within which to address decentralization is evident in Bank support for local governments. Support for decentralization through individual sectors in general is not sufficient to strengthen institutions and accountability systems that span different sectors at the local level. There is a need for high-level leadership and oversight of the process of designing Bank support to ensure greater coherence and consistency.

Overall, the quality of Bank support was of medium quality for the evaluation period, but it has improved in the last 15 years.

Chapter 3

Evaluation Essentials

- Decentralization frameworks improved in several respects following Bank support—substantially in 7 countries, modestly in 12, and negligibly in 1.
- The most successful aspects of Bank support for decentralization frameworks pertained to the legal frameworks for intergovernmental relations, the frameworks for intergovernmental fiscal transfers, and subnational financial management.
- Bank support was less effective in clarifying the roles and responsibilities of different levels of government and in improving own-source revenue mobilization by subnational governments, often because of lack of political commitment.
- Bank support brought better results when there was consensus around the reform within the country prior to Bank engagement and when the support was combined with incentives for local institutional reform.

Outside of the Parliament Building in Cape Town, South Africa. Photo by Trevor Samson, courtesy of the World Bank Photo Library.

Bank Support for Decentralization Frameworks and Subnational Government Capacity

A sound decentralization framework at the country level—defined throughout this evaluation as the full set of institutional arrangements within which decentralization is undertaken and sustained, specifying, among other things, how service delivery responsibilities and resource mobilization authority are apportioned among the various levels of government, as well as the associated accountability arrangements—must cater to a wide range of goals, from macroeconomic stability to equity.

The framework needs variously (depending on the country context) to ensure clarity in assignments, absence of unfunded mandates, reasonable stability in revenue assignment, effective budgeting and financial management at both the central and subnational levels, prudence in subnational borrowing and debt management, and adequate accountability of subnational governments.

Even where Bank support is significant, attribution of results to that support is a very challenging exercise. First, results are influenced by many variables, including local institutional capacity, political factors, and aid dependence. These variables are themselves difficult to measure. Second, the Bank is only one of many development partners that provide support; in several of the 20 countries, other development partners such as UNCDF, the Danish International Development Agency, and the U.S. Agency for International Development (USAID) supported decentralization, often starting before the Bank did.

In all the cases with high or substantial achievement of targeted results, Bank support was combined with strong government commitment to reform. These caveats notwithstanding, interviews with government stakeholders and development partners during field visits suggest that the Bank's superior knowledge of decentralization—based on the diversity of its experience in different country contexts, its ability to influence governments to seek policy reform, and its ability to provide attractive levels of funding—were all important for achieving progress.

Recognizing these challenges, this evaluation limited itself to assessing intermediate outcomes in areas where the Bank has provided support in these 20 countries.[1] The intermediate outcomes were grouped in two broad categories: strengthened intergovernmental relations and improved administrative capacity and accountability, each with three or four subcategories (see table 3.1). Given the varied starting points and contexts in each country, the evaluation assessed progress in these dimensions, using a before-and-after analysis.

Strengthening Intergovernmental Relations

Bank support to strengthen intergovernmental frameworks led to high or substantial progress in the achievement of intermediate outcomes in 8 of the 20 countries (table 3.1) and modest progress in another 9. The basis for this finding is explained below.

Strengthened legal framework

The development literature highlights the importance of a strong legal foundation to

Table 3.1: Assessing Results of Bank Support for Strengthened Intergovernmental Relations

Quality of results	Strengthened regulatory framework for decentralization	Receipt of more timely and predictable fiscal transfers by subnational governments	Enhanced framework for own-source revenue/discretionary resources of local governments	Improved framework for prudent borrowing and debt management at subnational level
High	• Key laws or regulations related to decentralization or intergovernmental fiscal framework (such as fiscal responsibility and subnational borrowing) passed or issued • Being implemented	• Improved institutional framework in place for intergovernmental fiscal transfers • Subnational governments receiving more timely and predictable funds	• Improved framework in place to enhance own-source revenue • Increasing availability of discretionary resources of subnational governments	• Rules for prudent borrowing and debt management strengthened and being effectively implemented at the subnational level • Improved access to prudent borrowing
Substantial	• Critical laws supported by Bank passed but implementation not begun	• As above, but subnational governments not yet receiving transfers in a fully predictable or timely manner	• Improved framework to enhance own-source revenue or own-source revenue of local governments increased as a result of Bank support, likely to be replicated and sustained in the future	• Framework for prudent borrowing established, improving debt management, although little or no improved access to prudent borrowing
Modest	• A few subsidiary laws passed, but critical areas still unregulated and subject to political or executive discretion	• No institutional framework in place, but donor funds being sent through transparent formula	• Some initial outputs in terms of framework or piloting of mechanisms, but no substantial improvement	• Clear rules for debt management, but debt management not improved and no change in access to prudent borrowing
Negligible	• Some policy dialogue but no output	• No difference in institutional framework, and no increase in timeliness or predictability in receipt of funds	• Reduction in own-source revenue, and no framework in place despite several years of policy dialogue and/or support	• No rules for debt management formulated, and no increased access to prudent borrowing

Source: IEG desk review.

ensure permanence and predictability of the institutional arrangements under which subnational governments function (see, for instance, Ahmad et al. 2005; Bird and Vaillancourt 1994; Boadway 2006; Shah 1998).

The legal framework for decentralization improved to substantial or high degrees in 12 of the countries studied. The piloting of implementation mechanisms through Bank-supported projects led to the significant revision of decentralization laws in Burkina Faso and the formulation of legislation in Rwanda.[2] Legal changes, supported by the Bank through DPLs, helped improve intergovernmental relations by deepening or fine-tuning fiscal decentralization frameworks (Ethiopia, Russia, and Uganda) or by establishing laws for fiscal responsibility and discipline at the subnational levels (Brazil, Andhra Pradesh and Karnataka [India], Pakistan, and Peru). In Ethiopia, Bank support contributed to clarifying the legal framework for functional assignment in *woredas* and municipalities.[3]

The Bank has also supported laws that have improved access to public information at subnational levels, thereby increasing the accountability of governments to their citizens. Several states in India passed right-to-information legislation with Bank support. Initial analysis suggests that commercial and government stakeholders are using these right-to-information systems more often than ordinary citizens are, but with increased awareness and capacity this measure can be a powerful instrument in helping shed light on local government decision making.[4]

In other countries, the new laws had only modest effects because of reduced government commitment to implementation or lack of consensus on the way forward. For example, in Tanzania, significant policy dialogue has only partly resolved conflicts between various legal enactments. In Albania, the Law of Prefects was passed with Bank support, but several other critical laws essential for establishing the decentralized framework were not passed during the evaluation period.[5] In Bolivia, the Bank waived a loan condition for legal amendments that should have clarified responsibilities across levels of government. In Nicaragua, although laws have been passed with Bank support, key aspects need to be amended.

Assuring legal rights to information is a first step to enhancing transparency.

Even when the government passed legislation to clarify the rules for decentralized governance, the evaluation found that the effectiveness of such laws was enhanced if the Bank simultaneously supported implementation of these laws at local levels by providing fiscal and other incentives for institutional and behavioral changes in the various sectors and levels of government.

Timeliness and predictability of transfers

The Bank supported improving intergovernmental fiscal transfer frameworks in 19 of the 20 countries. Bank support contributed to substantial results in seven countries and modest results in another five.

Bank support helped governments develop formula-based transfers in Ethiopia, Indonesia,[6] Russia, Rwanda, Pakistan, Uganda, and Sierra Leone. For example, in Russia (see box 3.1), reform has furthered the evolution of a clear and transparent system of transfers to regions; the government uses formula-based equalization grants, earmarked financial assistance for regional finance reform, and capital grants that are distributed competitively and require cofinancing.[7]

Support for legislation is not enough by itself; the Bank must help to provide incentives to enforce the laws.

In Uganda, although a formula has been developed and applied, most development funds are still earmarked by the central government. In response to increasing concerns about the limited autonomy of local governments, with Bank support the Ugandan government is implementing a pilot that gives 15 districts the flexibility to reallocate recurrent conditional grants within and between sectors.[8]

In Pakistan, with Bank support the federal and provincial governments established a fiscal framework to finance the district governments

Box 3.1: Good Practice in Russia

Decentralization reform efforts supported by the Bank during the late 1990s (including with three sector adjustment loans) were not successful, given the political volatility at the time. But a second set of Bank operations had better results.

The Bank first helped the government prepare the Fiscal Federalism Strategy of 2001 and supported the enactment of two laws to underpin the reform: the Law on General Principles of the Organization of Government in Subjects of the Russian Federation and the Law on Local Self-Government. The Bank also provided technical assistance and financed a system of performance-based grants that encouraged fiscal reforms by regional governments.

This appears to have resulted in greater clarity in the assignment system, instituted a formula-based transfer mechanism that allocated more funds to poorer regions, and provided incentives to subnational governments to reform their fiscal systems. These systems were later extended to government funds at the regional level, triggering significant reform of regional fiscal management as well as of the regional-to-local fiscal transfer system.

By 2003, about one-third of the Russian regions were using the formula-based transfer system and receiving funds in a timely and predictable manner. The status of federalism in Russia, however, remains unclear because of some recent political decisions, such as the presidency taking on the authority to appoint regional governors.

Source: Field visit to Russia (April 2007).

With Bank support, one-third of the sample countries have established formula-based transfers.

and facilitate the regular flow of funds. This has made more resources available at the subnational level.

In 7 of the 19 countries, allocations of government funds continue to be either discretionary or opaque. For example, in Albania the central government introduced a formula, developed with Bank support, that sets the amount of state resources to be allocated unconditionally to the local governments. The bulk of the development funds, however, continue to be distributed as conditional transfers that are arbitrary and negotiated. In other countries, progress is limited to a few sectors or to donor funds. In Tanzania, formulae for transfers are sector specific; more than 80 percent of the funds are earmarked, and the effective transfers of the budgeted funds to district governments are not always timely or predictable (World Bank 2006k).

Critical elements of transfer systems are yet to be addressed and remain discretionary or opaque.

In other countries, serious problems remain in the design of transfers. For example, mining resources in Peru are distributed based on the origin of the resource, which results in inequitable distribution. Also, municipalities in Nicaragua receive transfers but not clear or commensurate assignment of expenditure responsibilities.

In five countries, outcomes of Bank support have yet to materialize, in part because of the lack of a clear framework. Although the Bank began supporting urban and rural decentralization in Burkina Faso in the 1990s, that support has not led to the establishment of a clear framework for intergovernmental fiscal transfers given the country's predominant focus on deconcentration. As of June 2007, transfers to local authorities continue to be discretionary and based on a simple measure of population, which gives disproportionate advantage to the biggest and richest cities (World Bank 2007a). The results are similar in Madagascar (World Bank 2004c), where the policy direction may become clearer—decentralization legislation was passed in 2004—but a system of transfers has not yet been instituted. In the Philippines, support was provided mainly through ESW (ADB and World Bank 2004; World Bank 1994b)[9] and policy dialogue but has not yet led to discernible results.

Transferring large amounts of funding to municipalities and local governments without a clear strategy and without development of local capacity can reduce accountability. The evaluation found that it is important to support local governments with technical assistance to enhance capacity and accountability institutions. In some countries, Bank support has helped create incentives for fiscal and administrative reform at the local level, and this constitutes good practice (see box 3.2).

Additionally, such transfers should avoid the risk of softening the budget constraints that have been built up in several countries. Equity considerations are also important in determining the nature of transfers. In Bolivia and Russia, assessments have found that shifting more and more resources to departmental and municipal governments without equity considerations can lead to disparities in service delivery.

Own-source revenues

The literature on decentralization, including Bank ESW, suggests that when local governments raise their own revenue, they will be more autonomous from the central government and more likely to be responsive to their citizens for quality and efficiency in service delivery (Ter-Minassian 1997, p. 49; Taliercio 2005).[10] Bank support has aimed to increase own-source revenues at the local level in the 20 countries that were the focus of this evaluation, through policy dialogue, DPL conditions, or project support.[11] Desired results have, however, been difficult to achieve. (See figure 3.1 for data on distribution of resources in a set of six countries.)

The evaluation found no single best approach for addressing this issue. Bank support has varied in the five countries where it has contributed to improving the framework for own-source revenue. In the states of Bahia and Parana (Brazil) and in Nicaragua, Bank support helped enhance municipal own-source revenues through computerization of records, rationalization of tax rates, and increased efficiency of tax collection. In Brazil, the current transfer system to municipalities, however, has been identified as reducing states' incentives to collect own-source revenue.[12]

Lack of client consensus on direction has sometimes made change more difficult.

In Russia, Bank assistance supported the centralization of revenue administration. This has helped to improve intergovernmental fiscal frameworks through a more equitable allocation of resources among the regions. Since 2005, both tax assignment and transfer formulae have been refined in the Budget Code. This made the system more stable and transparent, although regions can no longer tailor the intergovernmental system to suit local conditions and have reduced incentives for

It is important to provide incentives for fiscal, financial, and administrative reform at the local level before transferring funds.

Box 3.2: Strengthening the Role of Local Governments

In about half of the country cases, including Karnataka (India), Russia, Rwanda, Sierra Leone, Tanzania, and Uganda, the Bank provided support directly to local governments to facilitate the implementation of decentralization laws and to initiate institutional reform through demand-based capacity-building programs. Typically, such support provides development block grants from the central government (through the budgetary system) to local governments for physical investments for mandated services that are their responsibility. Access to funds is contingent on a minimum set of institutional, financial, and operational criteria. Local governments that do not meet these criteria can have access to capacity-building grants to upgrade their institutions. Such an approach of direct support to local governments is critical for local service delivery and is now reflected in the CASs of about half of the study countries.

Although most projects are still open and it is therefore too early to assess results, the experience in Uganda suggests that the program has helped increase the number of district governments meeting the minimum capacity standards, leading to substantial institutional strengthening. For example, the program created an opportunity for the first-ever audit of lower local governments (below the district governments), which required the preparation of final accounts and identified some financial management problems. The field assessment found, however, that the regularity and scope of local audits has decreased because of a lack of funds after the project closed.

Access to information has been increased. Central governments receiving support are required to publish the amount of funds transferred to local governments in newspapers, and local governments are expected to post the amount of funds received on local council bulletin boards. Field assessments confirm that such measures have helped enhance transparency, with citizens monitoring financial information on budget releases (how much and when).

Bank support under this project has also supported the development of a cross-sectoral monitoring system of local government performance. However, the indicators will need to be strengthened during the next phase of the support.

Source: Field visits and Bank reports.

Figure 3.1: Distribution of State and Local Revenue Sources

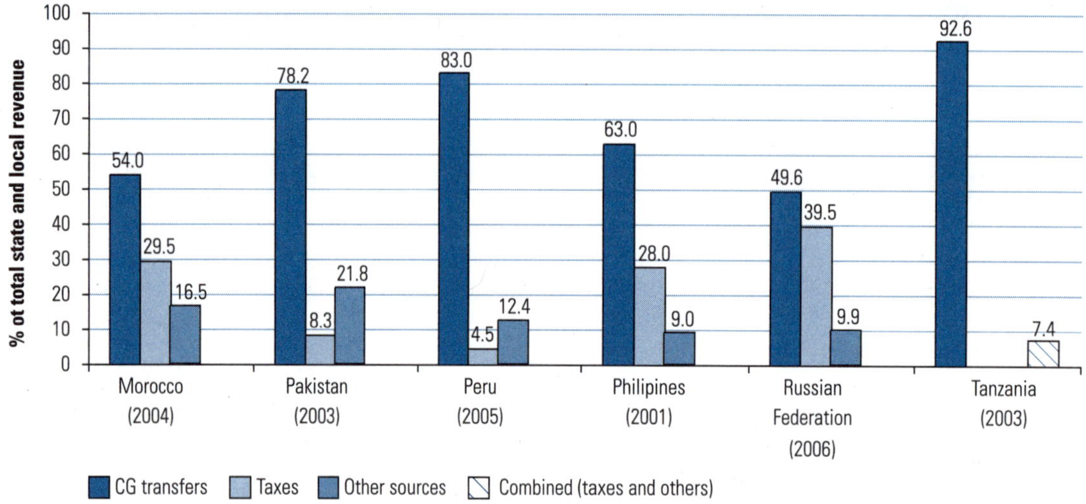

Source: IMF-Government Finance Services and World Bank data.

raising own-source revenue. Nevertheless, the evaluation found that this first step was a necessary condition for macroeconomic stability.

In Sierra Leone, Bank assistance helped establish incentives for local councils by providing them with a 50 percent matching grant for revenues raised locally.[13] However, for capacity and institutional reasons, revenue generation is still negligible, even though the framework is in place.

Enhancing frameworks for own-source revenue through Bank support has been difficult.

The evaluation found modest results in this area in eight country cases, for reasons that include inappropriate assignment of revenue sources, inefficient tax administrative systems, and weak local capacity. In Indonesia, where authority for local governments is granted under decentralization, new local taxes have proliferated (sometimes without a legal basis). Many of these taxes have little economic rationale and impose additional transaction costs because of their arbitrary nature and wide variation across localities. In Peru, municipal tax revenues increased by 11 percent in real terms because of Bank support for tax policy and administration reforms; however, local governments do not have discretion over revenues and the Congress determines all tax policy issues.

There has been little progress in increasing own-source revenue by local governments for various reasons, including inappropriate assignment of revenue sources and weak local capacity in tax administration.

In 7 of the 20 countries, results have been counterproductive. Own-source revenue of districts in Tanzania and Uganda[14] has diminished significantly since the Bank began its support for decentralization. In Tanzania, as discussed in chapter 2, this happened as a direct result of Bank support that centralized revenue sources while other Bank support was in parallel helping decentralize expenditure responsibilities. There is as yet no clear strategy for enhancing local government revenue, and district governments continue to be dependent on central transfers for more than 90 percent of their budget in both countries, although there is ongoing dialogue.[15] There is also some evidence that the high level of transfers discourages districts from collecting own-source revenue (World Bank 2006k, p. 6).

In sum, own-source revenue can help encourage autonomy and responsiveness of subnational governments in service delivery. But it has been difficult to progress on this dimension because of central governments' reluctance to relinquish control over lucrative taxes, the need to strengthen central tax collection in countries undergoing fiscal stress, and the weak capacity and political will of many local governments to administer taxes. In the interim, however, enhancing the efficiency and capacity of local governments to use the resources they get from the central government and to collect local fees and taxes while engaging in policy dialogue on appropriate revenue assignments—as the Bank is doing in some cases—may be the best alternative.

Debt management and borrowing

The Bank has engaged in debt management and the regulatory framework for prudent borrowing at the subnational levels in only 8 of the 20 countries. (In the other 12 countries, this was not an immediate issue, with local governments receiving only grants and not being in a financial position to access credit.) The framework for subnational borrowing was substantially improved in four of these eight countries: Brazil, India, Russia, and Pakistan.

In both India (Karnataka and Andhra Pradesh) and Brazil, the Bank helped governments deepen their understanding of center-state fiscal issues through a series of informal notes, policy dialogue, reports, conferences, state-level ESW, and support for reform "competition" across states. With the passage of state fiscal responsibility laws in Karnataka and Andhra Pradesh in and around 2003, a clear limit to state borrowing was established. Although it is too early to assess the impact of the laws and sort out causality, fiscal positions have improved in the two states (see figure 3.2).

In Uganda and Tanzania, own-source revenue of district governments decreased after reforms.

Adjustment lending to the Brazilian central government, underpinned by good analysis, supported a package of reforms to the intergovernmental fiscal system. The center of these is the Fiscal Responsibility Law, which has strong enforcement mechanisms through the legal system.[16] The fiscal performance of the states and municipalities has improved since the 1990s, and the aggregate subnational sector has had primary surpluses since 2002. The approach in Brazil also represented good practice in that the package included support for central government incentives to states for adjusting their fiscal policies.

Raising efficiency and capacity of local governments along with policy dialogue for appropriate revenue assignment may be the best alternative.

Figure 3.2: Trends in Fiscal Deficits in Selected Indian States (as a % of gross state domestic product)

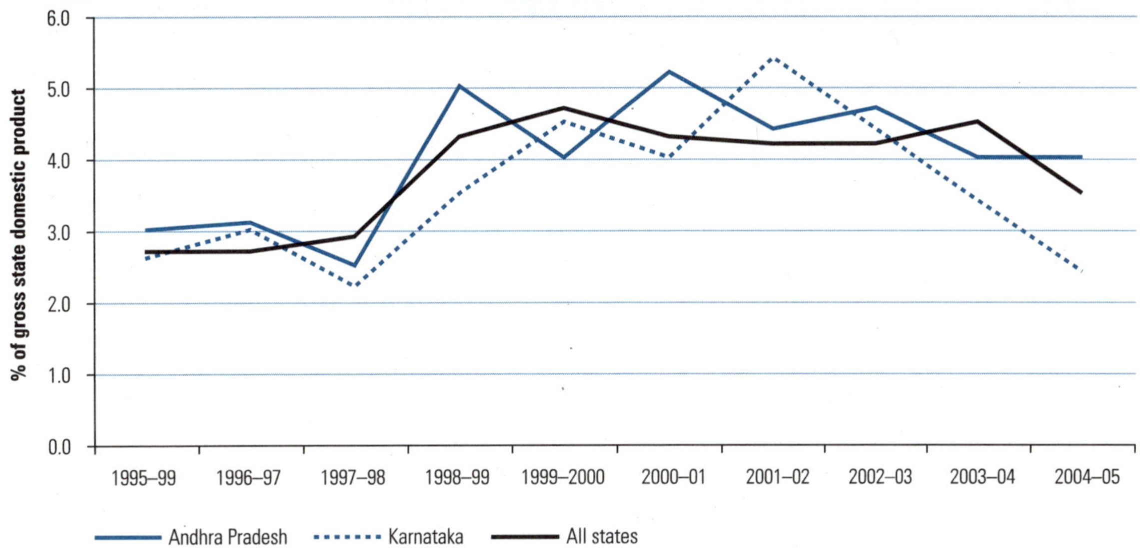

Source: Reserve Bank of India (various years).

In Brazil and India, states improved their fiscal positions through reforms, with strong support at the national level.

In Russia, Bank support helped establish a framework for subnational government debt management. Since 1999, Russia's regions have been able to borrow externally only to finance external debt incurred in the past. No new external borrowing is permitted, although the regions can borrow internally under certain conditions. There are credit-rating agencies, and 20 regions (of a total of 89) have received credit ratings. Bank support also helped Pakistan to pass the Fiscal Responsibility Act and improve debt management of provinces by substituting lower-interest for higher-interest debt.

Ensuring transparency of debt accumulation is an important first step in debt management.

Results of Bank support for subnational debt management were mixed in Albania, Bolivia, Peru, and the Philippines. For example, in Peru, despite recent legal measures,[17] a Bank study to assess the magnitude of subnational debt stock and identify municipalities that might face debt stock problems showed that unregistered debt is significant and that debt is highly concentrated. Moreover, a significant number of municipalities do not comply with the Fiscal Responsibility and Transparency Law (Ahmad and García-Escribano 2006, p. 21). In the Philippines, the Bank supported the development of a financing framework for local governments in 1996, but the implementation remains weak.

Thus, support for a strong framework to regulate subnational debt has proven valuable, where it has been undertaken with commitment at the national level and accompanied by improved financial management (including transparent debt recording) at the subnational level. In countries where subnational borrowing is not yet common, it may be wise for the Bank to support establishment of mechanisms for hard budget constraints and financial management processes for transparent debt recording.

Administrative Capacity and Accountability

Weak local administrative capacity and accountabilities result in less efficient service delivery and misuse of public resources (Shah 1998; Litvack and Seddon 1999; Ahmad and others 2005). To guard against this, subnational government capacity can be strengthened through administrative decentralization or free-standing capacity-building activities. The Bank focused mainly on the latter route to support decentralization, perhaps because of the complexity of civil service and administrative reform, particularly in a decentralized context.[18] IEG therefore examined the extent to which Bank support resulted in clearer definition of roles and responsibilities of different levels of government, stronger subnational financial management and procurement systems and capacity, and better systems to monitor and evaluate subnational government performance.

Box 3.3: Analytic Support to South Africa

Successful interventions are not necessarily expensive or linked with lending, say Bank staff who worked in South Africa (not among the 20 country cases covered in depth, as there was no Bank lending to the country) as it embarked on establishing a decentralized form of governance.

Three international experts financed by the Bank engaged key decision makers at workshop sessions and helped them prepare policy documents. Those papers provided the basis for significant aspects of the final legislative enactment. First, the vertical division of revenues between national and subnational levels has progressively shifted in favor of the latter. Second, ad hoc and opaque transfers that were a vestige of the apartheid era were phased out and replaced by more transparent and equitable intergovernmental transfers. Finally, the Bank supported the government in establishing a sound framework for subnational borrowing.

Source: Desk review and interviews with staff.

Bank support enhanced administrative capacity and accountability substantially in 7 countries, modestly in another 12, and negligibly in 1 of the 20 country cases. Box 3.3 illustrates how the Bank's analytic support helped the South African government design and implement intergovernmental reform.

Roles and responsibilities of different levels of government

It is important first to clarify the service delivery responsibilities of each level of government, define the necessary competencies, and then establish the expenditure and revenue responsibilities of each level (see World Bank 2004j, p. 185).[19] Lack of clarity in responsibilities has reduced accountability and hampered the effective operation of subnational governments, particularly where subnational governments depend on central government transfers.

Even capacity building has been difficult where the responsibilities were unclear. Although the Bank has addressed this issue in all 20 countries through analytical support or lending activities, substantial results are readily apparent only in Ethiopia, Russia, Pakistan, Rwanda, Sierra Leone, and Uganda (see table 3.1 on page 30).

Support for prudent subnational borrowing must be accompanied by transparent debt recording at the local level.

In Russia, Bank support helped clarify responsibilities at each government level and strengthened institutions for implementing decentralization (through improved coordination and linkages between central and local institutions). Similarly, in Pakistan, terms of partnership between different levels of government have helped clarify the roles of various actors in the health and education sectors. In

To strengthen administration at the local level, Bank support focused on institution and capacity development.

Table 3.2: Assessing Results for Enhanced Administrative Capacity and Accountability

Quality of results	Improved clarity of administrative responsibilities of different levels	Strengthened financial management and procurement capacity at subnational levels	Improved monitoring of subnational government performance
High	Improved clarity in responsibilities of different levels of government established by law and being implemented	Improved financial management institutions (external audits, accounting standards and reports, and internal controls) and improved transparency in procurement at subnational levels	A well-functioning monitoring system of local government performance with relevant data being available at all levels of government for improving policy decision
Substantial	Clarification being improved by project-related arrangements generating improvement in overall system	Strong and sustainable institutional changes with limited outcomes but evident or clear likelihood of improvement in both cases	An effective monitoring system initiated at project level and planned to be replicated for a more general level
Modest	Some outputs (say responsibilities clarified for one level), but confusion continues at other levels and in overall arrangements	Improvement only in one area or mainly outputs such as relevant laws, but no evidence on improvement in external audits, accounting standards, or transparency in procurement	M&E system of local government performance is available in a sector (mainly through project-level assistance)
Negligible	No progress in this area	Some initial outputs in both cases	Some outputs, such as a framework for a monitoring system or a needs assessment, being undertaken

Source: World Bank documents.

Lack of clarity about responsibilities reduces accountability and hinders effective operation.

Uganda, Bank support to local governments helped clarify the roles of the various local actors as well as strengthening the links between different levels of government (see box 3.4).[20]

Other countries in the sample had less success clarifying the assignment of responsibilities among different government levels. Even with Bank support, governments have been unable to reduce the ambiguity in the roles of different actors involved in service delivery in Bolivia, Burkina Faso, Indonesia, Morocco, Madagascar, Peru, and the Philippines. This is partly because these countries have multiple players at the central and local levels, some with devolved functions and others with deconcentrated functions in the same sector. In several cases—Albania, Andhra Pradesh and Karnataka (India), Peru, the Philippines, the Republic of Yemen, and Tanzania—Bank support has sometimes contributed to confused allocation of responsibilities through its support for approaches that create parallel institutions for development activities at the local levels.

Box 3.4: Appointment of Chief Accounting Officers in Uganda

In the initial decentralization, the District Service Commission appointed all technical staff at Uganda's district level, but a 2005 constitutional amendment gave responsibility for the appointment of the chief accounting officer (CAO) back to the central government. Although this was widely perceived as having derailed devolution, field visits and interviews with government stakeholders and CAOs found that the latter are able to act more independently and fearlessly than the local commission.

The centralization of such appointments has reduced the risks of collusion at the local level between the executive and the elected council and facilitated better governance. One CAO noted that she was able to monitor and bring to light without any resistance a case where misrepresentation between a school and local district staff had led to payment of per capita funds for 1,500 students instead of the 250 actually registered. Citizens do not hesitate to bring cases to the CAO, because he or she is perceived as independent. This shows how selective division of authority can enhance accountability.

Source: Desk review and interviews with Bank staff.

Achieving clarity in the roles and responsibilities of different levels of government can be politically charged. A first step, therefore, would be systematic and publicly discussed analytical work to help stimulate demand and build consensus for reform within the country. Such analysis can then guide the selection of entry points for lending support. The Bank may also, as it is increasingly doing, improve clarity through project-specific mechanisms such as performance agreements or terms of partnerships between different levels of government.

Financial management and procurement capacity

The aim of Bank support in all 20 countries was to strengthen financial management and procurement systems and capacity at the subnational levels through one or more activities. Such capacity is critical to effective and transparent local resource management, especially when demand-side accountability mechanisms such as citizen participation and oversight are weak or nonexistent. In 75 percent of the countries, assistance to strengthen financial management systems was based on Country Financial Accountability Assessments and Country Procurement Assessment Reports that examined fiduciary issues at the subnational levels.

Bank support contributed to strengthened financial management capacity of subnational governments in a high or substantial way in 15 of the 20 country cases—making the subnational accounting and auditing systems more standardized and transparent. In Pakistan, Bank support has helped improve the timeliness and accuracy of financial statements, with annual accounts being produced within six months of the end of the fiscal year and improved reconciliation levels across governments. Roles of provincial and district accounts committees have been clarified, although capacity development has been slow because of the shortage of skilled staff for the district accounting offices. In Brazil, the quality of fiscal accounts information has improved continuously, reducing reporting delays and expanding the number of government entities (especially municipalities) that send fiscal reports for inclusion in the consolidated public accounts.

The Bank was less successful in supporting procurement reform; substantial results were achieved in only four countries, with modest results in the others.[21] Substantial progress in public procurement occurred in Parana and Bahia (Brazil), the Philippines, Kazan (Russia), and Uganda. Even in these countries, there is significant need for capacity building at the subnational levels (see IEG 2006e). In others, such as Pakistan, Tanzania, and the Republic of Yemen, there is little evidence of increased transparency and economy in local public procurement, although several outputs (particularly laws, regulations, and procurement agencies) have been generated.

Two factors have reduced the effectiveness of Bank-supported capacity-building programs. First, in many countries, personnel incentives and governance arrangements (such as levels of remuneration, transparency in appointment, and conditions of employment) have not been modernized. Trained staff, such as auditors and accountants, continue to shift to private sector jobs, so it is not clear that public sector service delivery benefits from their enhanced skills.

Second, the proliferation of local districts, often for political reasons, has compounded capacity issues in countries such as Albania, Brazil, Indonesia, the Philippines, and Uganda. This tends to increase administrative expenditures, exacerbate weak administrative capacity, and reduce resources available for service delivery. The political difficulty of reform on these dimensions has often stymied reformers, even with Bank support.

The Bank also supported pilot mechanisms to help strengthen financial management systems and government processes (see box 3.2, page 33). These include accreditation systems in Peru, which set out the objectives, criteria, and assignment of responsibilities that govern the accreditation of subnational governments so they can assume the management of decentralized programs. In Pakistan, contractual agreements between different levels of government contributed to reform of financial management systems. These programs, however, have relied completely on donor funds, and their sustainability with regular budget financing is untested.

Bank support contributed to substantial results in financial management in the majority of sample countries.

Monitoring subnational government performance

Monitoring local government performance requires (i) tracking the flow of resources from the central level to the local level and monitoring the fiscal performance of local governments (which is particularly justified when the former is providing the resources) and (ii) citizen oversight of local government performance in the actual service delivery. The second aspect is discussed in chapter 4.

Bank support for improving procurement was not often effective.

Monitoring the efficient use of public resources by local governments is essential, where local governments have a particularly fair degree of autonomy. It helps improve efficient allocation of resources, increase transparency in the use of public funds, and create accountability among different levels of government as well as among citizens. In 5 of the 20 countries (Brazil, Russia, Rwanda, Sierra Leone, and Uganda), Bank support led to improved systems to monitor the transfer of resources through the budgetary processes as well as to initiate some monitoring of local government performance.

In Brazil and Russia, stakeholders note that such transparent monitoring has improved fiscal discipline. For example, as a result of the Fiscal Responsibility Act in Brazil, the national government improved its monitoring of state and municipality fiscal performance.[22] Russia developed a good system to monitor regional budgets. All regions are required to submit information on 10 indicators regularly to the federal treasury; penalties for noncompliance include reducing transfers.

More lucrative private sector jobs and proliferation of local government structures have reduced capacity at local levels.

Progress has been slow in this dimension in other countries receiv-

Centralized monitoring of local government performance is essential, especially if subnational governments depend on transfers.

ing Bank support for decentralization. Some monitoring systems are not fully in place, or if in place, the systems still do not generate adequate information. In Peru, they are still confined to top-down monitoring at the central level. In Tanzania, monitoring is still only done for the donor-funded program, and it is still difficult to know how much funding local governments are supposed to receive and whether the funds have been released. In Indonesia and the Philippines, monitoring or reporting systems do not yet provide information on local government performance, although there is ongoing discussion on how this can best be undertaken (IEG 2007h, chapter 3). In Pakistan, systems are in place but are weak (World Bank 2007h, 2007i, 2007j).[23]

There is a need to develop robust indicators to monitor the costs of delivering services at the local level.

In addition to supporting measurement of access and quality of outcomes within each sector, the Bank needs to support the central and local governments in developing monitoring systems to measure the performance of local governments and the costs of delivering basic services. Recent local government support activities provide an opportunity to develop and test such cross-sectoral systems (see box 3.4). There is, however, still a need to develop robust indicators and mechanisms for measuring and monitoring LGU performance that take into account the diverse conditions and capacity levels of local government. Such monitoring systems would also facilitate provision of incentives for better performance and would increase transparency and accountability of local government functioning.

Overall Findings and Lessons

Bank support for decentralization has been associated with more successful results in areas where the central government is a primary driver:

- Enactment of laws
- Top-down improvement of financial systems
- Imposition of hard budget constraints.

Bank support generated weaker results in areas that require effective collaboration among multiple sectors across different levels of government:

- Enhancing own-source revenue of subnational governments
- Clarifying responsibilities of different levels of government
- Establishing cross-sectoral monitoring systems at local levels.

Better results have occurred in countries where Bank and other donor support was framed around a country-led strategy for implementing decentralization (see table 3.3). In the absence of a country-led strategy, Bank support often was fragmented and failed to recognize the important linkages between different policy actions affecting decentralization. Without such a country strategy up front, which may not be possible in all cases, Bank support for decentralization was more effective when initiated as smaller-scale interventions that allowed client stakeholders to realize the benefits of such reform (Sierra Leone, Russia, and Uganda) and strengthen their ownership of reform before scaling up.

Analysis of the case studies yields six main lessons for improving Bank support for decentralization frameworks:

1. Undertake upstream analysis, as has been done in Russia and South Africa (box 3.3), and help prepare an implementation strategy or plan that carefully considers all elements of decentralization and their linkages.
2. View support for decentralization as a package of fiscal, administrative, and governance reforms affecting different levels of government with the potential to influence different sectors. The Bank may then decide to provide assistance selectively in one or two areas where it has a comparative advantage and may agree that development partners will address other critical areas.
3. Prepare for a long-term commitment to implement successful decentralization strategies.

Table 3.3: Contribution of Bank Support for Decentralization Frameworks

Country traits for most of the evaluation period	Countries			
	High	**Substantial**	**Modest**	**Negligible**
Countries where there was greater clarity in policy objectives for decentralization and Bank support was provided consistently with country's stated objectives	Russia, Uganda	Brazil, Ethiopia, Pakistan	Philippines	
Post-conflict countries	Sierra Leone, Rwanda			
Countries with less clarity in policy objectives and/or where Bank support was not provided consistent with client objectives for decentralization			Albania, Bolivia, Burkina Faso, India,[a] Indonesia, Madagascar, Morocco, Nepal, Nicaragua, Tanzania, Peru,	Rep. of Yemen

Source: World Bank database and IEG review.

a. In India, results of support for fiscal reform in the states of Andhra Pradesh and Karnataka would be considered substantial; support for local governments generated modest results in terms of decentralization. In India, although political decentralization is strong, there is considerable ambiguity in the devolution of functions because of resistance to implementing fiscal and administrative decentralization. In Indonesia and Tanzania, although the laws exist, there are evident weaknesses in terms of inconsistencies between laws and weak implementation of administrative decentralization.

As needed, package support into manageable phases across CASs, reflecting a clear sequencing of Bank activities with monitorable indicators.

4. Form joint partnership strategies with other development partners to ensure complementary roles.
5. Support capacity building at central and local levels, tailoring it to the responsibilities and roles of each level of government.
6. Use a judicious mix of instruments to support decentralization.

In 80 percent of the countries where Bank support generated substantial improvement in decentralization frameworks, DPLs helped encourage policy reform. DPLs also tended to encourage a shift from a multiplicity of investment projects with different sectoral approaches to more consistent, systemic support. They also allowed for more effective collaboration within the Bank and among development partners than other approaches would have done. They also allowed countries to take ownership.

Better results are associated with Bank support that was aligned with a coherent country strategy for decentralization.

Budget support was more effective in sustaining policy reform when there were accompanying investment loans that had a framework consistent with the DPLs. They helped build necessary institutions and create ownership of the reform at local levels (Uganda and Russia).

Chapter 4

Evaluation Essentials

- Support for decentralization in the education sector was more effective when the country had a clear framework for decentralization.
- Understanding the country context was critical for successful outcomes.
- Bank project assessments rarely monitor the effects of decentralization on service delivery.

Fada school children, Chad. Photo courtesy of Kimberley Fletcher; FletcherGallery@Mac.com.

Bank Support for Decentralization in Education Services: A Sector Example

Did Bank support for decentralization of education services have intermediate outcomes that are likely to improve service delivery? The education sector was selected for deeper review because of a recently completed IEG evaluation in this sector (IEG 2006a), which included a few in-depth country case studies.[1]

Additionally, there are ongoing IEG evaluations in health, water, and municipal management sectors, which are likely to examine some sector-specific and decentralization issues. Six country cases (Morocco,[2] Pakistan [Province of Punjab], Peru, the Philippines, Russia, and Tanzania)[3] were selected for analysis based on (i) regional representation, (ii) those that received Bank support for decentralization, and (iii) those where missions were undertaken and/or where there were recent IEG evaluations.

This chapter points to some initial lessons in designing Bank support for decentralization in the education sector. In each case, the evaluation focused on the three intermediate outcomes specified in the evaluation framework (figure 1.1 and see table 4.1).[4] It did not evaluate the delivery of services itself (one of the final outcomes in the framework) because of the paucity of data on project outcomes at the local levels and the difficulty of attributing Regional or national-level outcomes to Bank support for decentralization.

In three of the six countries (Pakistan, Russia, and Tanzania), Bank support was provided within the context of overall client agendas for decentralization. Legislation in each country had transferred responsibilities for service delivery to lower levels of government before the implementation of Bank support reviewed for the evaluation. Here, Bank support aimed to rationalize the decentralization already existing in the county, using its assistance as an entry point.

In three of the six countries, the governments had enunciated decentralization policies covering the education sector; in the others, Bank support tried to develop a decentralization framework.

In the other three countries (Morocco, Peru, and the Philippines),

Bank support explicitly attempted to create a normative framework to initiate decentralization, using its assistance in the sector as an entry point. In Morocco[5] and Peru,[6] the government had not yet decentralized education when Bank support in the sector was prepared. In the Philippines, the sector was already partially decentralized and Bank support aimed to deepen this.[7]

Improving Intergovernmental Fiscal Frameworks in the Education Sector

Bank support helped improve intergovernmental fiscal frameworks for education in Russia, the Province of Punjab (Pakistan), and Tanzania, consistent with the prevailing framework within the country. In these three countries, local governments receive funds in a more transparent and predictable manner than before the Bank-supported reform, thereby ensuring availability of resources for service delivery in this area. Field visits in Tanzania and Chuvashia (Russia) confirmed that schools have been able to deliver services in a more competitive and efficient manner since decentralization (see box 4.1).

In Punjab, Russia, and Tanzania, the Bank helped enhance predictability of transfers.

Introducing an element of competition in fiscal transfers has helped improve the delivery of education services in Russia and initiate reform at the local levels. The fiscal transfer system resulted in schools competing for enrollments by improving service quality. The allocation of resources on a competitive basis to regional governments willing to initiate and implement reform has been noted as enhancing local ownership and accountability for improving service delivery. In contrast, in the Province of Punjab (Pakistan), the allocation of funds to schools has remained arbitrary and opaque since decentralization.

Per capita fiscal transfers to schools led to competition in improving service delivery.

In Tanzania, local governments acted more as agencies with delegated rather than devolved responsibilities. Responsibilities are still shared between the Ministry of Education (which is unwilling to give up its control) and the Ministry of Local Government, with the Ministry of Finance being the conduit for external development assistance. Education funding for the district arrived from multiple sources, and there was weak coordination between central, regional, and district administration in the delivery of primary education.[8] District education officers had to answer to the ministry representatives as well as to the district executive director. Stakeholders identified education funds with the central government and donors, rather than the district budget. Thus, although Bank support helped increase the availability of resources at the local level, it only modestly enhanced local governments' decision making, responsibility, and accountability.

Table 4.1: Assessing Results in the Education Sector

Consistency with client's intergovernmental fiscal framework	Enhanced administrative capacity of local governments in education	Improved accountability to citizens
• Improved predictability and timeliness in receipt of funds, consistent with intergovernmental fiscal transfers • Strengthened roles of different actors, consistent with decentralization framework or stated objectives of Bank support	• Strengthened capacity of local government staff and school managers or administrators • Increased control of teachers by local governments or their powers delegated to facilities	• Improved school autonomy, consistent with client's decentralization framework • Strengthened oversight by parents and citizens • Established minimum service standards or outcome monitoring through development of national learning assessments

Source: IEG desk review.

In Punjab Province, with budget support from the Bank, a system of annual conditional grants for education has been initiated between the provincial and district governments, based on a needs-cum-performance formula. The grants are provided on signature of "terms of partnership" agreements signed by both governments. These agreements help improve the transparency and efficiency in the financing and management of the education sector by clarifying the responsibilities and obligations of districts and the province in planning and implementing projects. However, subsequent transfers to schools remain opaque and are yet to be addressed.

In Morocco, Peru, and the Philippines,[9] where Bank support did not have the benefit of a government-led decentralization framework, the Bank supported delegation of some education responsibilities to local governments. However, these efforts did not generate the expected results. In Morocco, school construction and some decision making were decentralized to provincial governments (when Bank-supported efforts to decentralize the responsibility to community groups failed), but even the transfer of project funds to provinces proved to be difficult.

In the Philippines, the assumptions underlying rapid decentralization of education management to LGUs proved to be overly optimistic, particularly because Bank support attempted to introduce new roles at the local level in a sector not fully devolved under the 1991 Code. In Peru, political economy issues were not fully analyzed, and Bank support for decentralization of education included in the project was dropped.

Local government roles under Bank support were not always consistent with government policy.

Enhanced Administrative Capacity of Local Governments

The evaluation focused on two administrative aspects: strengthened systems and capacity for monitoring results at the local level, and capacity building of local government staff and school administrators to improve their performance (see box 4.2). The Bank supported decentralizing the appointment of school staff only in Punjab, Pakistan (among this six cases in this chapter), where DPLs supported measures to enable local school councils to hire additional "contract" teachers based on merit. In the other five countries, the focus was on improving capacity of teachers and their efficient deployment. There was little systematic assessment of outcomes in this area.

The Bank helped to clarify roles and responsibilities through agreements signed between different levels of government.

Bank support for decentralization in the sector was not as successful in countries without a broad decentralization strategy.

Box 4.1: Aligning Fiscal Transfers with Local Sectoral Priorities

Piloting fiscal transfer systems within the country's broad decentralization framework was effective in **Russia**. Bank support helped pilot regional governments adopt the legal frameworks necessary for per capita funding and replace funding according to cost or staffing levels. All schools in participating regions now receive resources according to funding norms, linked to reform in the sector.

This has improved competition by creating demand among students for better-quality services. It also helped schools increase the own share of resources from 11 to 17 percent between 2001 and 2005. A presidential directive has been issued to implement per capita funding across the country, signaling the perceived success of the system, although other regions have the autonomy to determine whether to implement the decree.

In contrast, in **Tanzania**, despite significant results in education outcomes in quality and access, intermediate outcomes from a decentralization point of view were not fully effective. Development funds were transferred through formula-based grants directly to schools through local government budget accounts, but the central government continued to provide detailed instructions on their specific use, which limited scope for local government decision making (except to a small degree in the procurement of textbooks). Thus, the ability of local governments to play a meaningful role in local sectoral reform was not strengthened.

Source: Field visits and Bank reports.

Box 4.2: Gender and Capacity Building at the Local Level

Decentralization in traditional societies may lead to a revival of patriarchal approaches in governance at the local level. One way of mitigating this risk is to strengthen the capacity of both women and men to participate in local-level decision making or user groups and to ensure gender-balanced training in terms of both content and access.

Research shows that mandated representation of women in local leadership can help policy decisions to be more gender aware (Chattopadhyay and Duflo 2001); field assessments in the Philippines and Uganda confirm the benefits. Such measures are prevalent in the education and water sectors and in social fund and community-driven development (CDD) activities:

- In Tanzania, school committees are gender balanced and democratically constituted. Training includes all stakeholders, male and female. Issues of HIV/AIDS, gender, and governance are mainstreamed into all training.
- In Pakistan, the Bank supported close monitoring of gender-segregated education data. The appointment of teachers is based on a point system, which includes some affirmative action for recruitment of women. School councils were reestablished in fiscal 2004 based on majority membership of parents, with mothers represented in councils of girls' schools, although significant capacity constraints limited their participation.
- In the Philippines, IEG field assessments of Bank support in the water sector found that women felt empowered by their participation in water user groups and noted the new skills and competencies they had developed as meter readers, lay auditors, and lay accountants.
- In Indonesia, Bank support has resulted in improved opportunities for women's participation in drafting local development proposals; self-assessments suggest that women have become more empowered. Fifty-three percent of the loan proposals approved were from female applicants.
- In Uganda, under the Bank-supported Local Government Development Program, 28 percent of trainees and 30 percent of the beneficiaries of short-term jobs were women. The impact of these activities has not been measured.

Much more could be done to better monitor whether decentralization is benefiting men and women equally through improving outcome indicators of monitoring systems. The lack of gender-disaggregated data at all levels poses a significant restraint to understanding whether Bank support for decentralization has resulted in different results for men and women.

There is also need for a gender focus in middle-income countries outside East Asia. Bank support in these areas often seems to take a gender-blind or—at best—a gender-neutral approach.

Source: Field visits and Bank reports.

Assessment of capacity-building support was mostly focused on outputs.

In Russia and Tanzania, Bank support led to enhanced capacity at the local level in ways that improved service delivery. Field visits in Tanzania confirmed conclusions in Bank reports that training communities and local governments had improved their ability to play their new decentralized roles in the education sector. In addition, an assessment by an independent nongovernmental organization (Hakielimu 2005) found that about 90 percent of schools reported receiving some training for school committee members, although they received only 50 percent of the intended amount allocated to each school.

In Russia and Tanzania, field visits suggest that there has been substantial capacity strengthening at the local level.

The assessment found that school recordkeeping was well organized and straightforward and noted that "council and school-level institutions have, to a large extent, performed as planned." It found evidence that suggested "improved efficiency and effectiveness, and also that capacity-building activities were also effective" (Hakielimu 2005). In Chuvashia (Russia), school managers and local government staff noted that training workshops organized by the Bank, in particular the World Bank Institute, had raised their capacity to deliver services.

In the four other countries, results were not as evident. In the Philippines, although there was progress in training sector staff at the local levels, the IEG mission found multiple agencies mandated to strengthen local government capacity; training tended to be supply driven and agency specific. Given the multitude of players in the sector, both at the central and subnational levels, and the lack of clarity in their roles, appropriate capacity building was not possible.

Despite the creation of a training department at the provincial level in Punjab, there is no evidence that these efforts led to more independent or responsive local decisions. Government employees said that although the federal government rushed to spend and raise social indicators, large programs could not be delivered successfully in the absence of adequate capacity and accountability.[10] In Morocco, in-service training of teachers and school principals was shifted to regional governments, but there is no information on outcomes.

Strengthening local systems and capacity to monitor performance and outcomes in their limited jurisdiction helped enhance not only accountability of local governments and service providers, but also local administration (see table 4.2). In Chuvashia (Russia), the regional government prepared and published an annual report on education, based on formats developed with Bank support. These annual reports generated local demand for reform and helped schools obtain local funds to pay for reform. This experience is being disseminated through inter-regional workshops, and other regions may replicate the preparation of such reports.

In Punjab, Pakistan, local efforts to monitor progress in education are still at an early stage, although the partnership agreements include specific and annually updated targets for each district, including input, output, and outcome targets. This is likely to lead to better data in the future.

Where multiple agencies are mandated to provide training at the local level, coordination is important for effective capacity development.

In contrast, in Tanzania, despite significant Bank support for capacity building, there is still no systematic institutional monitoring of education results at any level—central, district, or school. In Peru, Bank support financed the publication of both international and national assessment results; established monitoring and supervision systems, including the creation of a payroll system to track the problem of ghost teachers; and developed an M&E system designed to provide transparency of information during the decentralization process. Despite this, the efforts for institutional strengthening and capacity building have remained focused at the national and central ministry level and have not affected the local levels (IEG 2007e).

Monitoring local outcomes and performance helps enhance demand for reform.

Enhanced Accountability of Local Governments/Schools to Citizens

The evaluation examined the extent to which Bank support helped increase accountability at the local level by enhancing the voice of citizens in service delivery, increasing transparency in local government functioning, and supporting systems for holding local governments accountable to citizens. In terms of improved citizen voice and

Table 4.2: School Autonomy and Accountability in Three Pilot Regions in Russia Supported by the Bank

	Pilot regions					
	Samara		Chuvashia		Voronezh	
Progress	**Planned (%)**	**Actual (%)**	**Planned (%)**	**Actual (%)**	**Planned (%)**	**Actual (%)**
Independent bank accounts opened	100	**100**	55	**61**	70	**70**
School boards established	90	**90**	70	**84**	65	**100**
Introduction of PCF	**Done**		**Done**		**Done**	

Other achievements

- PCF was also introduced in 22 "grant" regions against 7 planned.
- A legal framework for implementation of PCF has been adopted.

Source: World Bank 2007i.
Note: PCF = per capita funding.

Effective accountability involves enhancing citizens' voice, increasing transparency of local government performance, and establishing systems to hold local governments accountable.

transparency of local functioning, the evaluation found better results in the Philippines, Tanzania, and Russia, but such results were not evident yet in Morocco,[11] Punjab (Pakistan),[12] or Peru (despite significant efforts) (IEG 2007e, pp. viii, 10, 27).[13] Results were more mixed in the last area in all six countries.

Bank support sought to strengthen citizen participation and oversight of service delivery in the education sector in all six countries. In Tanzania, Russia, and the province of Punjab (Pakistan), school boards or councils have been constituted with Bank support, and these have been strengthened through capacity building and provision of some operational resources. Field visits in Tanzania found a relative increase in community support for such decentralized citizen oversight systems. In Russia, however, this was not a strong element (perhaps because of the need to change mindsets, as explained by a Russian nongovernmental organization). A 2006 USAID field assessment in Pakistan (USAID 2006) found that significant capacity constraints and lack of awareness hindered effective citizen oversight.[14]

Involving citizens in school management and procurement improved accountability in the Philippines.

In the Philippines, Bank support included the design of a five-year school improvement plan in partnership with the parents and the community. It used systematic data such as student achievement (based on school, division, or national tests) and language needs. This contributed an impetus for local planning and programming and helped empower school heads to manage a portion of the school resources and oversee capital improvements of their buildings. An innovative initiative for school heads and civil society groups to monitor procurement and delivery of school textbooks (textbook counts) and furniture also led to better economy and efficiency in the procurement of school supplies; it also engaged students and parents in oversight.[15] Although sustainability is a concern, these measures helped facilitate citizen monitoring of service providers and reportedly has led to some quality improvement.

Enhancing access to information for citizen oversight has generated positive results, though they will be fully exploited only with improved capacity and awareness.

Enhanced access to relevant information is important for citizen oversight and voice, as well as to enhance transparent functioning. In Tanzania, school and district authorities are expected to publish on public notice boards their respective budgets, the funds received, and their expenses. Field assessments in the Philippines and Tanzania found that citizens knew that information was available. Field visits to a few schools found that there was some information on several notice boards, although it was not always posted in a user-friendly format. The complexity of the transfer processes and multiplicity of funding sources reduced transparency and the accountability of local governments to citizens.

Improved transparency in financial management at the school level in Russia and Tanzania helped increase accountability of school managers both to governments and to citizens. Independent bank accounts were opened by all participating schools in these countries. In contexts of weak budgetary control mechanisms, the accounts also acted as a basic financial control mechanism, helping ensure that funds were used for the intended purposes.

Finally, the Bank has also helped client stakeholders pilot several instruments, such as Public Expenditure Tracking Surveys and citizen report cards, which have successfully helped identify leakages in the system and increase understanding of the perceptions of citizens on service delivery (the Philippines and Tanzania). These instruments have engaged poor people in an assessment of service provisioning and quality. They have typically generated valuable information that has led to some strengthening of accountability measures (see IEG evaluation of how to build better systems of M&E [Mackay 2007, box 9.1]).[16]

Bank efforts were not as prominent in attempting to strengthen systems for citizens to hold governments accountable and to seek redress in case of grievances.[17] Where they were addressed, Bank support was not effective.

Bank efforts helped establish a standard of minimum service in the education sector only in Tanzania, but this has not yet influenced the accountability of local governments because of the lack of systematic monitoring of their performance. In Peru, the 2007 Bank study on education identifies the lack of standards as a key reason for ineffectual accountability of schools. National learning assessment tests also help citizens and others to rank and compare the performance of local governments.

Bank support facilitated the participation of Russia in international learning assessments, helping compare the quality of Russian education with that of other countries. In Peru and Pakistan, the Bank supported national education assessment systems that could have contributed to increased government accountability. However, in both countries, specific responsibilities of different levels of government were unclear, leaving accountability difficult to establish. Moreover, these assessments were donor financed, raising concerns about sustainability.

Bank support for mechanisms to seek citizen redress of grievances has not been enough to increase local government accountability in any significant manner. Except in Lima, Peru, where a national toll-free complaint line has been established for the education sector, such systems have not been a common element of Bank support in the evaluation country cases. In all other countries, citizens use informal systems, such as complaint boxes or raising grievances at community meetings. Interviews in Tanzania with local government officials suggest that such complaints have led to some action (such as dismissal of errant teachers), but none of these systems has been systematically assessed.[18]

Conclusion

Although generalizations are difficult from such a limited sample, the above results do reiterate the finding in chapter 3 that Bank support for decentralization is likely to be more successful when it is aligned with a client strategy for decentralization. For example, Bank support for decentralization for the education sector in Russia and Tanzania was more successful because the interventions were designed within broader government decentralization strategies that included the education sector.

School accountability was strengthened through a variety of internal control mechanisms.

In contrast, in Morocco and Peru, the absence of a broad decentralization strategy hindered Bank efforts to support sector-specific measures to improve decentralization of education.[19] In the Philippines, although Bank support helped introduce greater school autonomy, the role of the local government in delivering services is still unclear and yet to be effective. In the Punjab, although there was a client strategy, the pace of the reform initiated by Bank support, combined with low capacity at the local levels, may have reduced the effectiveness of the support.

In implementing school-based management in decentralized countries, the roles of local governments should be clarified.

Based on a variety of research findings, the Bank has a preference for school-based management with active citizen or parent oversight and some monitoring by local governments. Unless such decentralization is planned carefully and the roles of different actors at the local levels are clearly defined, such school-based autonomy can cause tensions. This has been the case where responsibility for primary education has been devolved to local governments, as in Tanzania, or even where such decentralization is partial, as in the Philippines.

Efforts were usually less successful when the Bank team set overly ambitious objectives and did not fully consider the specific challenges of the country context. In some countries, for instance, the targeted spending levels required for Bank support exceeded the institutional capability, particularly at the local levels, even when the appraisal document noted the lack of implementation capacity. Analysis of the merits and demerits of decentralization in education was also weak.

In Peru, the Primary Education Quality Project included a component originally designed as a key tool to promote the decentralization of the

Bank support needs to increase attention to strengthen the accountability of local governments to citizens.

education sector, but it was modified before loan signature by a new administration. The new administration focused on improving school management while maintaining a centralized system. The Bank moved forward anyway, dropping the decentralization-related activities but not modifying the project objectives. The lack of strong technical analysis seems to have constrained the Bank from convincing the new government of the benefits of a decentralized system.

In strengthening the accountability framework at the local level, Bank assistance has been more successful in enhancing voice and transparency. However, it will need to improve its attention to mechanisms for holding local governments accountable. Strengthening focus on monitoring systems that provide comparative information across localities, establishing service standard benchmarks, publishing outcome data at the local level, establishing systems to redress complaints, strengthening local-level justice and accountability institutions, and encouraging some competition between governments can help increase such accountability. This is a complex task and will need close coordination among different units within the client country and the Bank.

Local data on service delivery are important; measuring regional or national outcomes is inadequate.

Finally, even this limited review stresses the need both for sector-level data at the local level and for such information to be available consistently across all local government jurisdictions. First, it is difficult to assess the impact of decentralization at the local level by measuring national or even regional outcome indicators in the sector. Policy makers need such data to fine-tune policies. Second, availability of local information can enhance responsiveness and accountability of local governments as well as generate local demand for reform when capacity is built up.

It is difficult to link decentralization to improved service delivery in the areas of education. For decentralization to work, the WDR (World Bank 2004j) notes, "There must be relevant information about performance across jurisdictions so that citizens can bring justified pressure to bear on politicians and policy makers if their area is lagging. Second, there must be an environment in which local jurisdictions can experiment and evaluate new approaches."

By these criteria (of the cases reviewed in this chapter), decentralization in the education sector has taken root only in Russia, in the sense that information across regions is being built up and regional governments and schools have significantly improved discretion over fiscal and administrative matters. In other countries, decentralization in the education sector has been initiated, but the central government continues to make the key administrative and fiscal decisions.

Chapter 5

Village meeting in Ilha Ibo, Mozambique. ©Atlantide Phototravel/Corbis; reproduced by permission.

Findings and Recommendations

For reasons as diverse as the countries themselves, decentralization is occurring in a broad cross-section of Bank-borrower countries. In several of the country cases reviewed, democratic governance and increased participation of local citizens in development planning through elected local governments are among the several objectives.

Findings

The election of local governments is the first step in this direction, and in all 20 countries this has occurred. From a development perspective, however, neither decades of theoretical and empirical research by academics nor the rich experiences of the Bank have shown that decentralization either facilitates or undermines the main goals of the Bank's assistance: to improve governance and service delivery while combating poverty and encouraging growth.

The evaluation found that the process of implementation is difficult in several countries that are under fiscal stress and that have regional inequities because of trade-offs that need to be made. Field visits indicated that decentralization has led to a sense of empowerment among local communities (Tanzania, the Philippines, and Uganda). But the evaluation also found that devolution under certain conditions exacerbated interregional inequities, as in Bolivia and Russia. Moreover, given the potential for elite capture, enhanced discretion for local governments was not always consistent with enhancing service provision for the poorest and most peripheral populations (in Pakistan and Peru). Thus, from a development perspective, decentralization is neither inevitable nor inherently good or bad, and Bank support must depend on country context, political will, and government commitment (see table 5.1).

Additionally, decentralization was largely driven by political motivations in many client countries. This fact led to the Bank's initial hesitation in supporting broad-based decentralization—including support for strengthening local governments. This in turn led to a sector-by-sector approach for decentralization, with a focus on efficiency. As a new wave of decentralization persisted, the Bank started to provide support more regularly.

From a development point of view, decentralization is neither inevitable nor inherently good or bad.

This is true especially since the mid 1990s, mainly because the process of decentralization resulted in shifting responsibilities to local governments in many critical sectors or subsectors, such as primary education, basic health, and water. It then became essential to ensure that decentralization was effectively managed, that resources

Table 5.1: Support for Decentralization Needs to Be Country Specific

Levels of decentralization	Possible Bank responses
The client has a legal framework for decentralization that has devolved or delegated responsibility and authority for service delivery to local governments and has established institutional arrangements for decentralization, although these may be weak.	• Align Bank portfolio with client policies on decentralization. • Support the client in analyzing the implications of decentralization across relevant sectors and different levels of government (covering macroeconomic fiscal effects, equity implications, administrative rationalization and capacity, accountability frameworks, important trade-offs, and critical political economy issues) if such analysis is not available. • Initiate dialogue on areas for further policy reform and support the client's development of an action plan for deepening reform around which development partners may provide coordinated support. • Help local governments strengthen their capacity for planning, budgeting, financial management, and procurement. • Strengthen accountability mechanisms of local governments to citizens and upward to higher levels of government as well. • Help the central government establish a cross-sectoral monitoring system to review local government performance and service delivery, with information made available to policy makers. • Ensure clarity in roles and responsibilities both vertically and horizontally, and strengthen administrative decentralization (whatever the mode may be). • Support testing or piloting of fiscal transfer systems to local governments, with some flexibility to respond to local needs and priorities. • Encourage appropriate assignment of revenue to local governments and strengthen capacity and systems to collect own-source revenue. • Ensure that hard budget constraints and transparent debt recording systems exist and work before encouraging local governments to borrow.
The client has decided to decentralize and/or has a policy or law but does not have institutional arrangements in place.	• Help the client analyze the costs and benefits of fiscal and administrative decentralization and examine different options. • Help local governments strengthen capacity for planning, budgeting, and financial management, as well as accountability mechanisms. • Help build a cross-sectoral system to monitor the results of service delivery at the local level. • Strengthen mechanisms for citizen participation in the design and implementation of development activities and strengthen the capacity of local governments to support such development. • Ensure coordination in any Bank-supported sector-by-sector decentralization and coherence across relevant laws. • Ensure hard budget constraints and transparent debt-recording systems before encouraging local governments to borrow.
Countries that are focusing on administrative deconcentration	• Avail themselves of existing sector-level or local level entry points that help the government strengthen human and institutional capacity at local levels. • Strengthen accountability of service deliverers to the government. • Support community participation in design, implementation, and monitoring of development activities. • Strengthen civil society monitoring at local levels to provide information on citizen perceptions of service delivery.

Source: IEG evaluation findings.

were available to fulfill the decentralized service delivery responsibilities, that capacity of local governments and other partners was strengthened to undertake the new responsibilities, and that local government accountability for service delivery was enhanced. Thus, Bank support for decentralization at the country level was highly relevant because it was responsive to client demands, consistent with their policies, and consistent with the Bank mandate to improve delivery of basic services to the poor.

The quality of Bank support for decentralization was mixed during the 1990s and was not always initiated in a timely fashion. However, the quality of support improved significantly in more than two-thirds of the countries in the last five years of the evaluation period. In these countries, the Bank has helped to undertake or update relevant and comprehensive analysis, identify fiscal costs and equity implications of decentralization, and support necessary policy reform. At the same time it has provided technical assistance and support to local governments to strengthen their institutions and their capacity to play their new roles. There is still a need to strengthen the Bank's results-based approach for decentralization, with a focus on assessing results at the local level and establishing causal links among inputs, outputs, and desired outcomes.

The evaluation found that Bank support contributed to improved effectiveness of decentralization in a manner that is likely to enhance service delivery, substantially in 7 of the 20 countries, modestly in 12, and negligibly in 1. The evaluation did not attempt to aggregate the indicators for quality and decentralization frameworks into a single rating. However, a comparison of the ratings for quality and results indicates that when the quality of Bank support improves, the results also get better (see table 5.2). This suggests that closer monitoring of the quality of Bank support for decentralization will likely improve the Bank's contribution to overall results in the country.

Much has been achieved, but this evaluation identified five broad areas of concern:

- Bank support brought better results where there was consensus around the reform within the country prior to Bank engagement.
- The achievement of results is hampered by the fragmentation that comes with a sector-by-sector approach.
- Assistance aimed at bolstering the basic decentralization framework in client countries is important, but equal attention is needed to strengthen capacity and accountability mechanisms of local governments.
- Analysis of political economy issues is critical to the prospects for success and sustainability of decentralization and, therefore, to Bank effectiveness.
- Systematic monitoring and evaluation of local outcomes is critical for understanding the impact of decentralization on local service delivery to the poor.

The Bank's support for decentralization was, at a sectoral level, driven largely by considerations of efficiency.

The quality of Bank support improved in two-thirds of the 20 countries in the last five years of the evaluation period.

Anchoring Bank support to country-led decentralization

Results have been better in countries where Bank and other donor support was framed around a country-led strategy for implementing decentralization (Uganda and Russia). In the absence of a country-led strategy, Bank support often was fragmented and failed to recognize the important linkages between different policy actions affecting decentralization.

Thus, for example, if a country implemented fiscal decentralization without clarifying authority and responsibilities at different government levels, results were weaker (Albania and Nicaragua). In some countries, after several years

Bank support was effective when it was linked to a country-led decentralization strategy.

Table 5.2: Better Quality of Bank Support Associated with Better Results

Quality of Bank support	Percentage of ratings for decentralization frameworks: High or satisfactory	Moderate or negligible
High (6)	5	1
Medium (14)	3	11

Source: IEG evaluation.

of weak results, the Bank supported the preparation of a strategy for implementing its decentralization policy (Madagascar and Nicaragua).

Overcoming fragmentation

Better collaboration across Bank units would enhance the development effectiveness of Bank support for strengthening decentralization. For example, in Tanzania, Bank support for the decentralization of expenditures by the regional urban unit and parallel support by PREM for centralization of revenue sources limited the effectiveness of overall Bank support for decentralization. In Nicaragua, collaboration between the agricultural and rural units, which supported a law of fiscal transfers to municipal government and PREM—which reportedly cautioned the government against the law—may have avoided some setbacks.

Separate analysis and interventions for strengthening urban local governments as opposed to rural local governments further fragmented support for decentralization in states in India. Improved collaboration between units working on different aspects of decentralization through sectoral interventions could have enhanced development effectiveness in Albania, the Philippines, and the Republic of Yemen.

Future Bank support needs to be designed as part of a broader framework for decentralization. Such support may be incremental and focused on specific institutions or on a particular level of government. The framework need not always be developed in depth in every sector, and different elements need not be pursued simultaneously. However, it should ensure that different sectoral interventions (including urban and rural) can be coordinated to avoid internal contradictions and to complement one another.

Better coordination between different units within the Bank that are providing support for decentralization would be helpful.

Bank country directors and vice presidents have the span of vision and control to avoid an isolated sector-by-sector approach. A few country directors have already begun to require more cross-sectoral collaboration in providing support. One Regional vice president has placed one unit in charge of developing a strategy to support client countries as they seek to strengthen decentralization in consultation and collaboration with relevant sector units. The Uganda country team holds weekly cross-sectoral meetings to discuss Bank support and to enhance consistency. Such practices need to be encouraged as governments move forward with their decentralization agendas; this could avoid harm that Bank support could cause without such coordination.

Strengthening local governments

The evaluation found that a broader agenda of intergovernmental institution building that encompassed local governments was lacking in almost half of the countries evaluated—especially those without decentralization plans or political consensus for innovative reforms. The evaluation found a need for support to strengthen local government systems. Once a country puts into place elected local governments and provides them with some responsibility for service delivery, it is important for the Bank to recognize them as legitimate agents of the local development process. Additionally, Bank support for local institutional reform needs to have solid intermediate benchmarks that will encourage results-based strengthening of local governments, both rural and urban.

The Bank needs to proceed with caution in client countries where some form of political decentralization has taken place but the administrative and fiscal details remain murky. Local governments should receive Bank funds as credits or block transfers only when that support is underpinned by thorough analysis. It should also be linked to technical assistance for local governments, strategic but incremental, and should be included within a strategy for decentralization reform. Additionally, as the Bank implements its local government program, it should mitigate the risk of softening budget constraints that have been carefully built up.

Understanding political economy issues

Finally, the evaluation found that the Bank's support was often insufficiently grounded in an understanding of the country's political economy, particularly at the local government level. Analytical work did not ask basic questions about the country context, such as, Which actors and interest groups have an interest in undermining reforms? Who has an interest in success? What are the ways in which actors will attempt to game the system in the future?

By comparing proposed or ongoing reforms with ideal best practice benchmarks, analytical work often did not assess whether the proposed reforms could create a sustainable political equilibrium. What looks like a sensible recommendation—such as encouraging local credit markets with limited central oversight or voluntary coordination among regional health agencies or local mayors, and so forth—might be unrealistic. Political economy factors must be reviewed from the beginning, which calls for an analytical framework that is not exclusively sectoral.

M&E at the local level

The impact of decentralization cannot be measured by Regional or national outcome indicators or by assessing inputs such as percentage of fiscal transfers or of own-source revenue of local government budgets. Robust local-level indicators and systematic assessment methods are urgently needed before one can judge the effectiveness of decentralization to improve equitable service delivery.

This is not an easy task. There is a paucity of data on resources needed for effective service delivery in different localities. Furthermore, the absence of institutional mechanisms for establishing and monitoring affordable minimum service standards even in basic education or health care also makes the task difficult.

In closing, it is also important to remember that much of the optimism about decentralization, in particular devolution and enhanced accountability, presupposes some degree of local revenue autonomy. Although generating local revenue is linked to the wider economy and is a long-term strategy, there is a need for a realistic understanding about how this will be achieved, especially in highly unequal countries. Much of the Bank's work on decentralization sidesteps this crucial issue.

Recommendations

Strengthening local governments in both rural and urban areas is critical when they are responsible for delivering basic services.

In many of its country programs, the Bank has made a de facto strategic decision to support decentralization and subnational government capacity development. In a few cases, notably where the client country has made decentralization a cornerstone of its development strategy and has demonstrated political commitment to decentralizing, Bank support has been built on an explicitly cross-cutting approach.

In most cases, however, Bank support has taken a sector-specific route, targeting decentralization and/or subnational government capacity development as a logical way of supporting more effective and responsive service delivery. In these latter cases, the various Bank sector units have not always provided consistent and coherent support for decentralization.

Looking forward, IEG offers the following recommendations. They are applicable to every client country that has transferred at least some responsibility for service delivery to subnational governments, where the Bank makes a de facto strategic decision to provide support for decentralization through either a cross-cutting or a sector-specific approach:

Improved understanding of political economy issues is essential to help frame more realistic and less ambitious objectives in this area.

- Ensure that Bank support, particularly lending, is underpinned by genuine client commitment to decentralized service delivery, given its importance to the success of Bank interventions. Occasionally, a role for the Bank may be justified in the absence of client commitment (for example, to forestall potentially adverse measures), although the evaluation finds that Bank interventions under such circumstances are not usually effective.
- Encourage the adoption of a more results-based approach to decentralization by helping develop in-country and Bank capacity for M&E

that focuses on local outcomes (such as enhanced accountability, greater citizen participation, and improved service delivery) rather than only on the process of decentralization.

- Ensure that Bank support at the country level is—among other things—
  - Founded on a clear analytical framework based on an integrative understanding of economic, political, and institutional factors at different levels of government and across sectors affected by decentralization
  - Accompanied by support (from the Bank or others) to develop and maintain local government capacity to the extent feasible.
- Strengthen institutional arrangements within the Bank to ensure that an integrative view underpins Bank interventions, particularly those based on sector-specific entry points.

Appendixes

Meeting of Mexican farmers. Photo by Giuseppe Franchini, courtesy of World Bank Photo Library.

APPENDIX A: TREATMENT OF DECENTRALIZATION IN BANK STRATEGIES AND POLICIES

IEG reviewed Bank strategies and Operational Policies to assess their treatment of decentralization-related issues.[1] Although several strategies discussed decentralization, no policy addressed the issue substantively. OP 8.60 on Development Policy Loans (DPLs) states, "The Bank may provide development policy lending to a member country or to a subnational division of a member country." OP 8.30 on financial intermediaries is discussed because it was found to have some relevance for municipal development funds. All safeguard policies apply to subnational lending, as do some other policies, such as OP 4.20 on gender.

Bank strategies have taken a variety of approaches to decentralization. Some acknowledge that decentralization is occurring in client countries and suggest the need to ensure involvement of lower-level institutions in capacity building and in making choices. Others, such as rural development, the previous Health Strategy, the Public Sector Strategy, and the Cities and Local Government Strategy, strongly encourage and support decentralization within their sectors while noting the risks.

The remainder of this appendix provides brief descriptions of these approaches. It is merely a "cut and paste" of relevant paragraphs from the strategies and policies with some care to ensure that the overall messages are not distorted.

A. Water Resources Sector Strategy: Strategic Directions for World Bank Engagement (2003)

This strategy focuses on local government and citizen participation in determining strategies and building capacity but does not suggest at all that this may be done by decentralizing water management. In fact, there is more of a suggestion that effective management may need decisions to be made at a higher level.

Water management must make a series of important transitions, including from local to regional and international management. Water management is moving from being just a local issue to being a national and an international issue, requiring new approaches to financing, dispute prevention, and resource management.

B. Sustaining Forests—A Development Strategy (2003)

A major Bank concern in the natural forest component of its program has been the prevalence of the concession system of management, which has produced great pressure on the resource and social and environmental problems in many places. Governance issues are at the core of this problem. In addition, the rapid trend toward decentralization in the countries will have consequences on managing the complicated, interconnected natural resource systems that will not necessarily be positive.

The policy seems to focus more on people and communities:

> To ensure that women, the poor, and other marginalized groups in society are able to take a more active role in formulating and implementing rural forest policies and programs; to support the scaling up of collaborative and community forest management so that local people can manage their own resources, freely market forest products, and benefit from security

> of tenure; to work with local groups, NGOs, and other partners to integrate forest, agro forestry, and small enterprise activities in rural development strategies.

C. Making Sustainable Commitments: An Environment Strategy for the World Bank (2001)

This strategy focuses on the ongoing decentralization in many countries and stresses the implications. A few examples:

> In parallel with the changing relative roles of the public and private sectors, the ongoing decentralization of regulatory functions from central to local government levels worldwide has increased the need for local government involvement in many areas of environmental regulation, and enhanced the role of civil society in influencing decision-making. The new challenges created by decentralization for effective environmental regulation and management at the local levels deserve special attention in capacity-building efforts.

A sample objective is the following:

> Supporting policy, regulatory, and institutional frameworks for sustainable environmental management. In cooperation with client countries and development partners, we will help client countries (a) strengthen their environmental policy, regulatory, and institutional frameworks with a special focus on local environmental institutions; (b) strengthen environmental assessment systems and practices; (c) reinforce the positive role of markets and the environmental benefits of sectoral and macroeconomic reforms; and (d) support good governance, institutions for collective action, increased transparency, access to environmental information, and public participation in decision making.

Its framework, however, indicates an increasing role of citizens, but not necessarily for local governments or decentralized institutions.

D. Education Sector Strategy Paper 1999 and 2007 Draft Update

Overall the 1999 strategy is noncommittal:

> *Governance and decentralization:* Virtually all of the Bank's client countries are tackling education reforms that often involve decentralizing management and accountability for results. The Bank plans (with many partners and leading academic institutions) to develop a training course for policymakers and international agency staff on what works and what doesn't and how to implement education reforms in politically sustainable ways.

> Arguments about the equity of local participation and the effectiveness of local decision making are often advanced to push for greater decentralization of the management of education systems. Central governments around the world have decentralized education management to varying degrees—and with different ends in mind. Some have delegated responsibilities to their own local representatives, while others have transferred authority to locally elected governments and, in some cases, to parent-elected school boards. Although they have a major role to play in education, governments cannot do everything. Fiscal considerations, including competing claims on the public purse, make it difficult for most governments—even those whose philosophies might push them in this direction—to be the sole provider of "free" education to all who seek it at every level. There are many areas of education service provision (such as textbooks and vocational training) where actors other than the government tend to be more effective and efficient.

The trend seems to be toward school-based management rather than a focus on strengthening local governments:

> Partnerships amongst central government, local government and communities, within a

more decentralized form of management, can improve service delivery; and poor communities and rural non-government providers can be effective partners in upgrading the quality of education. Local partners, in particular, have the local knowledge and the understanding of local values, culture, and traditions that are an essential feature of sustainable development.

Many others have important roles to play alongside the various levels of government. These other players include students, parents, families, communities, local and non-governmental organizations and foundations, teacher groups, various forms of private and public-private ventures, and numerous international organizations. The more this rich array of partners can work together effectively, the better the results will be — and the faster education will improve. Many partnerships are exemplary now, but some are not and most could be strengthened further.

2007 Draft Update

The trend toward decentralized management and financing of education has been gaining momentum. Decentralized management can improve local accountability but also lead to inconsistent roles of central, regional, and local authorities, as well as inequitable financing across communities. Policy reform toward effective decentralized service delivery is essential.

E. Reaching the Poor: A Renewed Strategy for Rural Development (2003)

This strategy strongly supports decentralization as part of good governance.

In the decentralization process, local governments must be given sufficient fiscal resources to discharge their new responsibilities. Political decentralization is also necessary, as it promotes accountability and governance reforms at the local level. This is especially important for rural areas because most rural people have had a weak political voice at the national level. The Bank will encourage governments to concentrate on: providing public goods; establishing legal, administrative, and regulatory systems that correct for market failures; facilitating efficient operation of the private sector; and protecting the interests of the disadvantaged. Decentralization offers great scope for improving delivery of public sector functions. Facilitating further decentralization in rural areas is an important part of the policy agenda outlined in the strategy. To promote the development of effective institutions for rural development, the Bank will support:

- Strengthening of local administrative capacity
- Transfer of responsibility for services to the administrative level closest to the users
- Enhanced accountability for public administration at every level
- Participatory approaches, including increased political space and participation in decision-making bodies for women
- Economies of scale in government functions
- Appropriate private sector involvement in the delivery of public services, with public accountability.

It also adopts community-driven development (CDD) as part of its overall strategy: "Decentralized development efforts such as CDD offer the potential for increased community participation in all aspects of rural development as well as offering greater inclusion of all social groups in rural decision-making." (See pages 35, 36, and 37 in particular.)

F. Reforming Public Institutions and Strengthening Governance: A World Bank Strategy (2000) (referred to as the Public Sector Strategy)

Decentralization is one of the eight key elements of the Bank's public sector strategy, and the strategy states its links with poverty alleviation as follows: "(i) increased resources for development purposes; (ii) improved service delivery; and (iii) empowerment of the poor to direct the use of government resources."

> We must prioritize our activities in order to staff effectively under current resource constraints. We aim for the Bank to be considered one of a very few leading authorities worldwide in several core areas where we have a track record or a comparative advantage, including (a) the role of the public sector, (b) the broad structure of government (including decentralization and intergovernmental fiscal relations), (c) core systemwide administrative and civil service reform and capacity building, (d) public expenditure analysis and management, and (e) sectoral institution-building (including regulation of private service delivery).
>
> Decentralization activity—an accelerating trend in many countries and the focus of extensive work in the Bank—entails a change in the legal and regulatory framework for government activity, and it often holds the promise of increasing both "voice" and participation (by moving the administration of public services closer to the citizenry) and competitive pressures (including competition among levels of government and between subnational entities). But while decentralization holds many promises, it also entails risks that must be addressed, including the risk of "capture" by local elites or lack of capacity within local government.
>
> Designing decentralization policy within a particular country context is a complex task. There is no right or wrong degree of decentralization or standard "best practice" that can be applied across countries, although most developing countries tend to be relatively centralized public sectors and could benefit significantly from greater decentralization if well-designed and implemented. The best design will vary depending on circumstances, and this complexity has sometimes been overlooked by the Bank and other donors in the haste to offer policy advice. Fragmentation of policy advice has also sometimes been a problem. Decentralization is a cross-cutting issue that affects most topics in which we engage our clients—from macroeconomic stability to service delivery. Although country teams are increasingly trying to bring a comprehensive, coordinated perspective, the traditional Bank approach has handled public finance and sectoral issues separately and has sometimes focused disproportionately on the fiscal aspects of decentralization without considering the political and administrative aspects that are critical to success.

See box 8 of the strategy for the Bank approach in the public sector. "This strategy paper does not go into detail in evaluating institution building efforts in particular sectors. That task should be a primary concern of strategy papers for the individual sectors."

G. Health, Nutrition, and Population (1997) and 2007 Healthy Development: The World Bank Strategy for Health, Nutrition, and Population Results

The previous Health, Nutrition, and Population (HNP) Strategy (1997) recommended that governments "be encouraged to address each of the three HNP priorities outlined above, through decentralization, greater partnerships with nongovernmental providers, and a more direct public involvement in securing sustainable financing." It states the need for sequencing:

> ...where institutional capacity for financing and regulation is weak, a gradual approach emphasizing decentralization and internal markets is better than actively transferring ownership of public facilities, with all its attendant employment and political consequences. In stronger institutional settings—when there is an appropriate and effective regulatory environment—a more active participation by nongovernmental providers can be encouraged.

The 2007 HNP Strategy takes a cautious approach to decentralization and only notes "taking advantage of decentralized decision-making and management while, simultaneously, putting in place compensatory mechanisms for capacity and equity issues." It suggests in its results framework that decentralization is one of the many innovative ways of making the system work.

H. Cities in Transition: Urban and Local Government Strategy (2000)

This strategy notes that decentralization is under way in all Regions and provides new ways to work together within the urban arena and with newly energized local governments. It stresses the need to focus on local governments:

> The role of national governments is being refocused to facilitate markets, promote economic and social stability, and ensure equity. But reforms of public sector management or private sector development will not do what is desired for national development until they are adapted and implemented appropriately at the municipal level. Local government remains the everyday face of the public sector—the level of government where essential public services are delivered to individuals and businesses, and where policy meets the people.
>
> The new urban and local government strategy does more than simply retool the urban development portfolio or seek stronger performance from it, although both are required. Rather, it argues for the Bank to recognize cities and towns as a dynamic development arena where the convergence of sectoral activities and collaboration among communities, levels of government, and other private and public sector institutions can create a microcosm of sustainable development for the country. The Bank would therefore apply to urban economies and local governments the same quality and rigor in analysis, advice, and strategizing that it applies to national economies and central governments. Ensuring well-functioning urban areas requires support to a spectrum of activities, both national and local, that affect urban outcomes. Skills and resources for this effort must be mobilized across sectors, thematic groups, and professional clusters in the Bank Group. The strategy therefore calls for a commitment by a wide coalition of forces within the institution and among external partners to working together in new ways on the urban frontier, with a newly empowered set of clients.
>
> The urban strategy is also geared toward helping government at all levels, the private sector (for profit and nonprofit), community groups, and citizens function in the urban economy in ways best suited to them. This means, for example, promoting effective competition among land developers and service providers; making local government budgets more transparent and thereby reducing the perceived risks of partnership for private financiers; increasing channels of information and collaboration among community groups, informal sector operators, and local government agencies; and refining policy tools such as targeted subsidies, basic land use planning, and urban transport management to address social and environmental externalities in the urban economy.
>
> With formal fiscal decentralization in many countries, the Bank's urban staff can bring the perspective of municipalities, and an understanding of the needs and constraints facing different kinds of local governments, into the national macroeconomic and fiscal dialogue to promote more effective design and implementation of these reforms.

The strategy clarifies that "an important feature of these efforts is the emphasis on strong underlying incentives for local government accountability, and performance, which are essential to combat problems of corruption." It notes that assistance for urban development has also "traditionally devoted attention to the intergovernmental assignment of functions, expenditures, and revenues that determines the system of incentives and the availability of resources for local governments."

I. Empowering People by Transforming Institutions: Social Development in World Bank Operations (2005)

The World Bank has consolidated its approach to social development into a single Bank-wide Strategy and Implementation Plan, entitled "Empowering People by Transforming Institutions: Social Development in World Bank Operations" (World Bank 2005d), which focuses on efforts to empower poor women and men through enhanced Bank support for social inclusion, cohesive societies, and accountable institutions. Social development is defined as transformation of institutions and, as such, promotes better growth, better projects, and better quality of life. The paper sets a vision, objectives, and a course of action for the longer term and suggests specific actions, targets, and institutional measures for the next five years. It clearly notes the need to link CDD activities with macro policies of decentralization and to integrate local governments into the CDD activities. Consequently, it proposes to reduce the bypassing of legitimate local governments and to ensure that Bank support for CDD activities is part of Country Assistance Strategy (CAS)–programmed strategies.

J. OP 8.30 on Financial Intermediaries (revised in 1998)

This OP is applicable to Municipal Development Funds:

> Financial intermediaries are inter alia to support private sector lending or to support the country's poverty reduction objectives. Financial Intermediary Loans are provided in the context of sound analytical work on sector issues, appropriate technical assistance, and, as relevant, development policy operations to address policy issues. Such FIs aim to remove or substantially reduce subsidies, whether provided through interest rates, directed credit, institution-building grants, or otherwise. Para 8 states certain conditions for poverty reduction programs including that they (a) are transparent, targeted, and capped; (b) are funded explicitly through the government budget or other sources subject to effective control and regular review; (c) are fiscally sustainable; and (d) do not give an unfair advantage to some FIs vis-à-vis other qualified and directly competing institutions.

K. Good Practice Note for Development Policy Lending: Subnational Development Policy Lending (2005)

This Good Practice Note is intended to provide guidance to staff in the preparation of development policy operations and is not mandatory operational policy. It provides advice to Bank staff and to government counterparts on development policy operations in support of state-level programs of fiscal and sector policy and institutional actions, with a focus on individual state development policy operations. The note complements the OPCS series of Good Practice Notes (World Bank 2004e) for development policy operations, particularly Good Practice Note 1, "Designing Development Policy Operations," and it also draws on earlier staff guidelines issued by the Poverty Reduction and Economic Management (PREM) Network. Development policy lending support for efforts to improve subnational finances, policies, and institutions takes different forms, depending on the roles of the central and the state-level authorities: fiscal federalism operations, multistate development policy operations, and individual state development policy operations. This Good Practice Note provides no advice on development policy operations supporting fiscal federalism reforms or on subnational investment operations (except when discussing the choice of lending instruments).

Section IV discusses the necessary assessments and criteria for determining when to lend to states or provinces, to whom to lend, and what lending instrument to use. With regard to intergovernmental fiscal relations, the note states:

> In the continued presence of a weak budget constraint in intergovernmental fiscal relations, a program to reform subnational fiscal policies is unlikely to be fully implemented or its outcome maintained over the medium term.... OP 8.60 requires "satisfactory fiscal relations with the central government" for subnational DPL operations to go ahead. The standard for "satisfactory" is not a textbook model of fiscal federalism—state responsibilities matching own revenues and rule-based transfers and binding constraints on borrowing—but a practice of fiscal relations that does not undermine the incentive for state fiscal policy reform.

Selection of Countries, Lending Activities, and Economic and Sector Work

Selection of country cases

All closed projects (as of December 2006) classified as having a decentralization or subnational theme were selected. These projects were then classified by country and Region. Bank-supported decentralization activities were found in 89 countries.

Twenty of the 89 countries were selected for the evaluation (table B.1), ensuring Regional representation (table B.2), as well as a mix of federal and unitary government structures. Some smaller countries and some postconflict countries were also selected. Some countries were selected in coordination with the IEG public sector reform and judicial reform evaluations. Together, lending to these 20 countries constituted about 47 percent of total lending classified as having a decentralization theme (table B.3).

Table B.1: Country Cases Evaluated

Albania	Madagascar	Russia
Bolivia	Morocco	Rwanda
Brazil (states: Parana and Bahia)	Nepal	Sierra Leone
Burkina Faso	Nicaragua	Tanzania
Ethiopia	Pakistan (Provinces of Sindh and NWFP)	Uganda
India (states: Andhra Pradesh, Karnataka, and Uttar Pradesh)	Peru	Rep. of Yemen
Indonesia	Philippines	

Table B.2: Number of Focus Countries

Region	Number of focus countries	Percentage of total commitment containing decentralization activities reviewed
Sub-Saharan Africa	7	42
East Asia and Pacific	2	59
Europe and Central Asia	2	36
Latin America and the Caribbean	4	41
Middle East and North Africa	2	50
South Asia	3	84

Source: World Bank data.

Table B.3: Activities with Some Decentralization Support, by Commitment, Fiscal 1990–2007

Instrument	Amount of commitment for decentralization ($ million)	Percentage of total commitment	Number of activities	Percentage of total activities
Development Policy Loan	10.498	47.6	63	31.0
INV	11.572	52.4	140	69.0
	22.07	100	203	100

Source: IEG sample activity list.

In the 20 countries, all lending activities approved after fiscal 1990 and closed by fiscal 2007 were reviewed in the public, health, education, urban, and water sectors to confirm whether they supported some aspects of decentralization (using the definition adopted for this study, see chapter 1). This resulted in a sample of 203 projects. About one-third of the identified activities involved Development Policy Loans (DPLs). The high percentage of DPLs can be explained by the increased use of the instrument for decentralization reform since the late 1990s and by the inclusion of some large loans to the Russian Federation, Indonesia, and Brazil.

Analytic Approach

All decentralization economic and sector work (ESW) (with significant analysis of decentralization issues) prepared for the 20 country cases was identified (more than 40 pieces). An external evaluator reviewed a third of the cases; the rest were reviewed by IEG evaluators. Indicators used for the assessment were as follows:

- Did the work discuss all aspects of decentralization (as relevant)? Did it discuss country-specific issues (political economy issues, fiscal costs of decentralization)? Did the ESW focus on issues related to monitoring and evaluation?
- Did the work reflect an understanding of what the Bank (and other key donors or actors) was doing in the area and recommend how the effectiveness of Bank support could be improved?
- Did the ESW provide clear and phased recommendations linked to the analysis?
- Were client stakeholders closely involved in the preparation of the ESW?
- Was the work undertaken in consultation with other donors?

The evaluation team reviewed 222 projects'/programs' (with significant decentralization components) appraisal and completion reports to understand how the Bank supported decentralization in the 20 countries. The analysis:

- Separated decentralization-related objectives (and classified them as fiscal, administrative, political, or purely capacity building at the subnational or local government level)
- Examined design issues, including (i) consideration of and addressing capacity-related risks; (ii) consideration of equity, gender, and environmental risks; (iii) consultation with local stakeholders and with other donors; and (iv) treatment of monitoring and evaluation indicators
- Examined achievement of stated objectives related to decentralization (used only for triangulating the country-level findings), based on information in the Implementation Completion Reports (ICRs), IEG reviews of ICRs and Project Performance Assessment Reports.

The evaluation reviewed **all country strategies during the evaluation period, decentralization-focused ESW,** and other activities to better understand how the Bank supported decentralization (decentralization frameworks and stated sectors) at a country level. This also helped the evaluators better understand the timeliness of response (mainly in terms of an ESW), framing of objectives at the country level, choice of instruments as reflected in country strategies, and whether the Bank focused on monitoring and evaluation in this area.

From the above analysis, the evaluation established **objectives of Bank support** in each country (thus mitigating the attribution issue).

The evaluation assessed the **quality of support,** using a three-point scale (high, medium, and low) to rate:

- Quality of ESW during evaluation period
- Bank support reflecting country-specific circumstances, particularly client participation in the design of Bank support, which was reflective of country context (identification of risks and how they were addressed) and of Bank diagnosis
- Internal consistency of Bank support at a country level
- Results orientation of Bank support
- Donor collaboration at country level.

The evaluation assessed **results in each country against stated objectives** in two areas, using a four-point scale to rate:

a. Decentralization frameworks
   i. Strengthened intergovernmental relations
   ii. Enhanced administrative capacity and accountability
b. Education and urban service sectors
   i. Generated resources for service delivery at the local levels, reducing reliance on local government transfers
   ii. Strengthened institutions, capacity, and incentives for improved service delivery
   iii. Improved accountability to citizens.

The **four-point scale** used to rate progress in each case was high, substantial, modest, and negligible. The rating was based on a before-and-after analysis. Indicators were aggregated to a country level for each area.

The evaluation did not aggregate the ratings for quality and decentralization frameworks to arrive at a single country-level rating for results, given that the final results of projects and programs are influenced by extraneous variables (such as wavering political commitment, for instance, caused by emerging political opposition) that are beyond the Bank's control.

Chapter 1

1. Subsidiarity is the principle that decisions about resource management should be made and executed at the lowest possible level if it can be shown that local capacity at this level is competent enough.

2. Management notes that, in its sector and thematic coding framework, sectors indicate which part of the economy receives support. Themes correspond to the goals of Bank activities. Both sector and thematic project coding are reviewed and validated centrally. Management maintains that decentralization, like environment, is a theme, that there are no known biases in assigning the decentralization thematic code to Bank activities, and that there are no pure investments in decentralization.

3. Activities focused on strengthening revenue sources and collection ability of urban governments, improving their efficiency, and strengthening their capacity for borrowing.

4. For example, in Tanzania during the 1980s, the IMF and the World Bank supported decentralization in favor of urban districts, particularly in Dar es Salaam, through the economic recovery program that supported policy reform for this purpose and through the water and sanitation project that provided support to the sector.

Chapter 2

1. A relevant ESW piece is one that discusses the implications of decentralization for the client's development agenda and makes appropriate recommendations.

2. The United Nations Capital Development Fund had financed a project that piloted the provision of support to local governments in a limited number of districts. The Bank, along with other donors, supported government actions to replicate the pilot in a larger number of districts and subsequently at the national level.

3. Management notes that Tanzania's Human Resources Development I Project, which the International Development Association supported with a credit, was by design not consistent with the Decentralization Act. The Tanzanian authorities designed it to explore alternative mechanisms for increasing local participation and better service delivery, notably in education. For that reason, the project was clearly labeled as a pilot. At completion, IEG rated it was satisfactory in terms of outcome, with sustainability rated as likely. The Tanzanian authorities adopted many of the elements of the pilot and integrated them into their existing decentralized structure countrywide.

4. See the project ICR (World Bank 2005a, p. 3), which notes that the decision to pursue the establishment of a regional health authority structure in the Tirana region (as part of a decentralization strategy) proved to be potentially problematic, especially given the lack of prior diagnostic or sector work. The Bank also supported the Health Insurance Institute that was eventually to develop into the sole purchaser of health care services from providers. See also the 2006 Albania Health Sector Note (World Bank 2006a), which concludes that such decentralization in Tirana calls for careful evaluation and corrective action based on the evaluation results (p. xii) This said, although IEG's ICR Review noted the confusion at the institutional level and proposed an audit, it also prematurely added that the project had laid the groundwork for a revised institutional architecture for a decentralized health system with the Ministry of Health as policy body and regulator, the Health Insurance Institute as insurer and purchaser of services and regional health authorities and planning (based on the Tirana Regional Health Authority model).

5. Similarly, the 2004 ESW report (World Bank 2004g) notes little progress in enabling local government access to private capital based on creditworthiness and notes that such finances are mainly sourced from development assistance.

6. The inability of private financial intermediaries to become depository banks for LGUs is a key structural impediment to their entry.

7. See the Project Appraisal Document (World Bank 2006i, p. 13), which notes that "loans and borrowing only account for 1.8 percent of LGUs' total revenue, and debt service only accounts for 2.8 percent of their total expenditure." More recently, a Joint IFC-World Bank Subnational Finance Department was established in 2007 to provide states, provinces, municipalities, and their enterprises with financing and access to capital markets—without sovereign guarantees. Such an initiative can perhaps provide a framework for lending to local governments within which both GFIs and private financial intermediaries can have a role.

8. In the Philippines, at the time of the IEG mission, decentralization was led by the regional urban unit, without the full benefit of PREM experts.

9. The Municipalities Law of 1997 lists a set of responsibilities of municipal governments but does not explain what is mandatory or specify a minimum set of obligations for municipal governments (World Bank 2003a, p. 11).

10. The Poverty Reduction Support Credit (PRSC) I included a prior action for the second tranche that would have required amendments to the Law of Municipalities to balance municipal expenditures with resources transferred to municipalities. The proposed presidential decree, however, could not amend the previous law, and the condition was therefore revised to allow a decree that would clarify some of the budget responsibilities of municipalities and help to neutralize the transfers to the municipalities. The PRSC II program document indicates that further progress in this area would be a priority for future PRSCs, including the presentation of a new law proposal to the National Assembly, as part of a revised strategy and policy.

11. Management notes that support from Social Development and PREM staff to Nicaragua on decentralization was well coordinated across operations. Staff from these networks worked together in supporting Nicaragua's Municipal Development Project, as well as the PRSC. The unexpected size of the transfers in the 2003 law did raise fiscal issues; strong cross-network integration was critical for the policy dialogue with government authorities to address not only fiscal issues but also local development priorities.

12. For example, the Ethiopia Rehabilitation and Social Development Fund Project established a centralized project appraisal and approval system under which local communities established community development groups to identify, seek financing for, and implement local development projects from a menu of choices. Local governments were limited to providing the recurrent costs of the completed activity and fulfilling some monitoring responsibilities. The funding went directly from the project office to the local community's bank account, and community groups undertook the procurement. Thus, although it is not inconceivable that the project had a positive, if indirect, impact on the capacity of local governments, it also provided for a lesser role for local governments in determining the allocation of resources than would otherwise have been given to them.

13. See, for example, Saxena (2003), which notes that although there may be benefits to both systems, there is need to sharpen the institutional links between political decentralization, in the form of Panchayati Raj, and administrative decentralization, in the form of user committees promoted by the external donor projects. Saxena adds that this is important because in several development projects, such as drinking water, health, watershed development, and primary education, government has relied on committees that are independent of panchayats. Often in the same Region, the World Bank has promoted different committees, one for forests, the second for drinking water, and the third for education, and most of these are distinct from panchayats. See also IEG's report on the effectiveness of World Bank support for community-based and-driven development (IEG 2005b, pp. 31–32).

14. The projects referred to in this paragraph are active and the results have not been assessed by IEG. Management in its response also pointed out that "a recent review of CDD and social fund activities in Africa showed that 71 percent of active operations transferred resources to activities that are undertaken through local government planning. In addition, two-thirds of these have local governments manage these CDD resources themselves."

15. The framework, developed by a group of development partners including the Bank, provides 28 high-level indicators to measure progress and monitor performance of PFM systems, processes, and institutions. They measure the extent to which the PFM system is an enabling factor for achieving development outcomes. The Bank has integrated the use of the indicators in PFM analytic work, as they facilitate structured measurement of progress.

16. Such joint diagnostic work has the potential to lead to harmonization of procedures, as is occurring in some countries, including Albania.

17. See the survey on support to local governance and decentralization (DEGE Consult and NCG 2006). The report notes that the dominant approach for delivering donor support for decentralization and local governance is still a project approach, where each donor supports a discrete project, with its own institutional arrangements for project implementation.

Chapter 3

1. For example, the evaluation does not assess whether the control of administrative staff was decentralized, which while an important area for decentralization, is one where the Bank has not provided much assistance.

2. In Burkina Faso, the Community-Based Rural Development Project and Urban Project II helped revise existing laws. In Rwanda, the Community Reintegration and Development Project laid the foundation for the government's approach to decentralization and the subsequent legislation.

3. Four regions and Addis Ababa have passed enabling legislation for municipalities with support from the Bank's PRSCs.

4. The effectiveness of the law will depend on how it is implemented. For example, the state of Karnataka issued a notification in 2005 to allow citizens to seek information henceforth only on one subject through a single application of less than 150 words. What constitutes "one subject" is left to the discretion of the Right to Information Commission. At the same time, there is a move to allow requests through electronic mail in the state of Bihar.

5. The Bank's 2004 ESW recommended as a medium-term measure "designing and implementing basic laws and regulations on local government." As a monitoring indicator for Bank PRSCs, "Basic laws and regulations on local government administration and fiscal autonomy passed." IEG understands that these laws were passed in February 2008.

6. The findings on Bank support for Indonesia are based on IEG's Country Assistance Evaluation: *The World Bank in Indonesia, 1999–2006* (2007g).

7. The first phase of the program was with Bank support (2001–04), but the government has since extended the program with its own funds.

8. There has been resistance from the education sector, where discretion is not allowed on the grounds that it may reduce the chances of meeting the Millennium Development Goals. During field assessments in Uganda, district chief financial officers reported that if the center realizes less tax revenue than expected, or if actual donor disbursements fall short of that budgeted, releases can often be delayed or less that that budgeted. Local government stakeholders noted the importance of monitoring fiscal gaps at the local level, which is the difference between the budgeted amount and that received.

9. See "Philippines Decentralization and Service Delivery" (ADB and World Bank 2004); see also 1993 Fiscal Decentralization Study and Devolution and Health Services (World Bank 1994a). The Philippines also participated in an ASEM grant for strengthening the policy framework for decentralization. In 2000, a public sector reform loan was initiated to help the government reassess the scope of decentralization in view and support the revision of the Internal Revenue Allotment formula with a view to improve its equity, incentives for local revenue mobilization, as well as its overall fiscal sustainability. Consensus was difficult to achieve on the intractable issues surrounding the Internal Revenue Allotment, and this activity was dropped.

10. See *Fiscal Federalism in Theory and Practice* (Ter-Minassian, 1997, p. 49). See Taliercio (2005): "The fact that subnational governments have both limited powers to raise revenues and limited capacity to collect them poses profound questions about the actual benefits of decentralization." See also http://www.worldbank.org/wbi/mdf/mdf1/revenue.htm: "Own-source revenues should constitute a very significant share of local finance. Governments spend more wisely and are more accountable for money they are responsible for raising." At a macroeconomic level, as discussed in chapter 2, encouraging own-source revenue at the local levels is also noted as being not without risks in contexts of fiscal stress (and where revenue generation is critical for the central government), weak capacity, or poor accountability (Raich 2005).

11. Such support has involved assisting Morocco and India (at a state level) to strengthen and implement the value-added tax framework and share the revenues, improving the policy framework for tax assignment in Albania, Bolivia, Ethiopia, Pakistan, Sierra Leone, Russia, and Uganda, and enhancing the own-source revenue of urban and rural municipalities through project-level assistance in several other countries.

12. Own-source revenues of subnational governments overall have not increased in Brazil.

13. The new fiscal decentralization policy introduces

criteria tax sharing with local government, for empowering local authorities to set tax and license rates and levy service fees, and for devolving property tax to local government. Legislation is pending to allow districts to collect revenue on property.

14. Field assessments in Uganda show that district governments are expected, for example, to cofinance the costs of several investment activities through their own-source revenue. When such revenue is not available, they divert transfers meant for lower levels of government to fulfill such obligations, and lower levels of government then get decreased funding.

15. A formula-based allocation of the General-Purpose Grant was initiated in fiscal 2005–06, although the final implementation of a formula for the General-Purpose Grant and the Local Administration Grant will not take place until June 2007. The Local Government Fiscal Review 2005 notes that the General-Purpose Grant has not compensated local governments adequately for the decline in own revenue sources.

16. Between 2000 and 2001, the Bank provided two adjustment loans in support of Brazil's fiscal performance and performance of the states in particular. The Program for Fiscal and Administrative Reform Special Sector Adjustment Loan—$505 million—consisted of policy actions that introduced and initiated the government's fiscal stability plan, implementation of the 19th amendment to the constitution. The second loan that the Bank supported for $750 million intended to deepen and improve fiscal reforms and supported the passing of the Fiscal Stability Plan and the Law of Fiscal Responsibility among other actions.

17. With Bank support, the government adopted and published a supreme decree requiring independent and publicized credit ratings of municipal and regional governments for them to borrow amounts above the ceiling established in the borrower's annual public indebtedness law.

18. In several countries, administrative devolution occurred (that is, subnational governments were given control over local staff, but the Bank was not involved in this decision [Indonesia, Pakistan, the Philippines, and Uganda]). In a few countries such as Morocco, Pakistan, and Nepal and sometimes through specific sectors such as in Bolivia, the Bank has tried to strengthen administrative deconcentration or decentralization, but overall such support has been highly limited, given the political economy issues surrounding civil service reform, with focus being more on containing the wage bill and on strengthening meritocracy in the civil service as a whole. See IEG's public sector evaluation (IEG 2008), which examines results of Bank support for civil service reform in general.

19. See WDR (World Bank 2004j, p. 185). Laws typically define broad responsibilities, leaving regulations to define competencies of each level of government and their expenditure assignments.

20. Field assessments in Uganda indicate that service quality is constrained by the ceilings imposed on hiring and offering competitive remuneration.

21. In several countries, Bank support has helped to pass or modernize procurement laws or establish procurement agencies. IEG, however, looked for evidence of results at the subnational level, without which the result was rated as modest.

22. As a result, states are regularly meeting their debt service obligations to the National Treasury and the latter continues to apply penalties to any states that fail to comply. The number of individual states generating primary deficits decreased from seven in 2001 to three in 2002 and to only one in 2003. In January 2003, for example, constitutional federal transfers were blocked when the state of Rio de Janeiro failed to meet its debt obligations. That state responded by restarting its scheduled payments.

23. See public financial management and accountability assessments conducted for different provinces in Pakistan (World Bank 2007h, 2007i, 2007j).

Chapter 4

1. IEG's primary education evaluation (IEG 2006a) reviewed decentralization and school accountability/community accountability, focusing on their impact on educational access, quality, equity, and learning outcomes. It found that decentralization and school accountability are not necessarily associated with improved access, quality, or learning outcomes, and may lead to inequities between poor and non-poor communities. In contrast, this evaluation of decentralization focuses on intermediate outcomes likely to improve service delivery (generation of discretionary resources for local governments for service delivery; strengthened institutions, capacity, and incentives for better service delivery; enhanced accountability of local governments to citizens for service delivery). It points to the lack of documentation of links between decentralization and better service delivery and finds that the desired intermediate outcomes were not achieved in three of the six cases reviewed.

2. Morocco, selected to ensure some Regional representation, is the only sample country where the findings are based entirely on a desk review.

3. Field visits also were conducted in Peru, the Philippines, Russia, and Tanzania. The evaluation also drew on field-based case studies of Bank support for primary education in Pakistan and Peru, conducted in 2006 as background for the IEG evaluation of primary education (IEG 2007d, 2007e).

4. This framework is consistent with the 1999 Education Sector Strategy and its 2005 Sector Strategy Update.

5. The 2001 CAS for Morocco relies on decentralization as a process that will help to reduce poverty, and specifically speaks about regional decentralization and community schools. The 1999 Policy Reform Support Loan included a prior action that required ministerial instructions to decentralize decision making in school mapping and project implementation to regional authorities. Bank investment projects supported decentralization of in-service training of teachers and school principals, budgeting and decision making to provinces, and school construction to communities.

6. The PSRL IV dealt with the decentralization of the social programs, and, *inter alia,* aimed to support the establishment of a clear legal basis for the decentralization of education and improve clarity in the roles and responsibilities of different levels of government. Other investment projects also supported decentralization in the sector.

7. In the Philippines, the 1991 Code did not devolve the education sector, although the construction and maintenance of school buildings was devolved to local government units. A Governance of Education Act focused on decentralization in the sector, namely through school-based management systems (see note 12 also).

8. These varying project and donor requirements led to one weak district in Tanzania (Kinodoni) having 950 bank accounts.

9. See endnote 3. The Third Elementary Education Project (TEEP) aimed to "introduce systems and procedures to decentralize selected education functions and the corresponding resources, to the Divisions and, where feasible, the schools"; and build capacities in support of decentralized implementation and effective schools. During negotiations, assurances were obtained from the government that it would carry out the project in accordance with the principles set forth in the Memorandum of Policy and with the TEEP Guidelines. It was agreed that decentralization to 26 provinces covered by TEEP will be given top priority. However, the decentralization was focused on a school-autonomy model for the most part.

10. See IEG (2007d, pp. 21–22), and IEG (2006c), which notes concerns of significant misuse of funds in the sector, pp. 6, 35–36, and footnotes 43 and 49.

11. See Basic Education Project ICR (World Bank 2004f). The focus of the project was to involve communities in the management of schools, but this was not achieved.

12. See Punjab Education Second Policy Development Credit ICR (World Bank 2006h).

13. See IEG (2007e, pp. viii, 10, and p. 27, footnote 24) and ESW on education in Peru (World Bank 2007m, chapter 9), which confirms that although there is great potential for voice of, and accountability to, parents, in reality accountability has not been built up.

14. See also USAID (2006), which found that capacity of local government staff had not been strengthened.

15. See the evaluation of the Bank's fiduciary instruments (IEG 2006e), which discusses the progress made in this area in the Philippines.

16. Some nongovernmental organizations in Tanzania protested to the IEG mission that steps taken to identify and address such leakages were inadequate.

17. This could involve measures such as establishing minimum service standards and holding national assessment tests to provide comparative benchmarks against which citizens can compare the performance of their government. It could also involve helping to establish pilot dispute-resolution mechanisms in the sector or to strengthen local-level accountability or justice institutions.

18. Strengthening local-level Parliamentary Accounts Committees has been tried in a few countries such as Pakistan, but has not yet had an evident impact on local governments. See also EU (2007, p. 73), where it notes that assessments have shown that citizen participation is important in extracting resources from local governments but less important in holding local governments accountable.

19. See Peru ESW (World Bank 2007m, note 17, p. 127), which concludes that "the state of decentralization in practice (and even in regulation) is fluid and confused to such an extent that it is impossible to make forecasts as to whether decentralization is likely to make all of the problems listed here worse or better." See also the Philippines PAD for National Program Support for Basic Education Project (World Bank 2006i, p. 2), which says that education remains "largely regulated by central prescriptions- administrative memos and orders." See also the

ICR of the Pakistan Second Social Action Program, which notes that "decentralization of powers could not be instituted in the social sectors alone in an otherwise highly centralized system of administration, in which lower level government functionaries were reluctant to exercise powers already delegated to them" (World Bank 2006h, p. 5).

Appendix A

1. The sector strategy outlines intent, discusses options, and presents arguments for adopting particular approaches. It provides nuanced guidance on the different actions that should be considered in different circumstances. An Operational Policy is intended as a more concise statement of the Bank's obligations to all Bank operational activities covered by the policy. It provides formal and accountable safeguard policies that are approved by the Board. The Operational Policy is accompanied by a definitions appendix and a Bank procedures document, which elaborate on some of the implementation requirements raised by the policy.

Acosta, Olga Lucia, and Richard M. Bird. 2003. "The Dilemma of Decentralization in Colombia." ITP Paper 0404, University of Toronto, Toronto.

ADB (Asian Development Bank) and World Bank. 2004. "Philippines: Decentralization and Service Delivery: From Promise to Performance—Cross-Cutting Themes in Local Government Functioning." Report No. 26104-PH, World Bank and Asian Development Bank, Washington, DC, and Manila.

AfroBarometer. 2006. "Delivery of Social Services on Mainland Tanzania: Are People Satisfied?" Briefing Paper No. 34, AfroBarometer, University of Michigan.

Ahmad, Ehtisham, and Mercedes García-Escribano. 2006. "Fiscal Decentralization and Public Subnational Financial Management in Peru." Working Paper No. 06/120, IMF, Washington, DC.

Ahmad, E., G. Brosio, and M. González. 2006. "Uganda: Managing More Effective Decentralization." IMF Working Paper 06/279, Washington, DC.

Ahmad, Junaid, Shantayanan Devarajan, Stuti Kehmai, and Shekhar Shah. 2005. "Decentralization and Service Delivery." Policy Research Working Paper 3603, World Bank, Washington, DC.

Aitken, I. 1998. *Decentralization and Reproductive Health*. Boston, MA: Harvard University School of Public Health.

Albana, Dhimitri, Belinda Ikonomi, and Majlinda Dhuka. 2007. "The Fiscal Decentralization Initiative for Central and Eastern Europe. Regional Development Policy Performance in Albania." http://lgi.osi.hu/publications/2007/368/FDI_Regional_Development_Albania.pdf.

Alonso, Rosa, and Robert Utz. 2003. "Fiscal Aspects of PRSP Implementation in Tanzania." http://siteresources.worldbank.org/INTPRS1/Resources/383606-1119904390686/bbl101204_tanzania.pdf.

Anderson, Jon. 1998. "Four Considerations for Decentralized Forest Management: Subsidiarity, Empowerment, Pluralism and Social Capital." Paper presented at the International Seminar of Decentralization and Devolution of Forest Management in Asia and the Pacific, Davao, Philippines.

Bahl, Roy, and Jorge Martinez-Vazquez. 2006. "Sequencing Fiscal Decentralization." Policy Research Working Paper 3914, World Bank, Washington, DC.

Baker, Jonathan, Hege Wallevik, James Obama, and Nazar Sola. 2002. "Local Government Reform in Tanzania: Towards a Greater Interdependency between Local Government and Civil Society at the Local Level." http://www.tanzaniagateway.org/contents.asp?cpg=8&topicId=17.

———. 2002. "Decentralization of Governance and Development." *Journal of Economic Perspectives* 16 (4): 185–205.

Ballivian, Ampara, and A. Spillmbergo. 2004. "Municipal Decentralization in Nicaragua: Fiscal and Institutional Issues." Policy Note, World Bank, Washington, DC.

Bardhan, Pranab, and Dilip Mookherjee. 2000. "Decentralizing Anti-Poverty Program Delivery in Developing Countries." University of California Center for International and Development Economics Research (CIDER) Working Paper No. C98-104.1, Berkeley, CA.

Bird, Richard M., and François Vaillancourt. 1994. *Fiscal Decentralization in Developing Countries*. Cambridge, UK: Cambridge University Press.

Bird, Richard M., Robert D. Ebel, and Christine I. Wallich. 1995. "Decentralization of the Socialist State: Inter-governmental Finance in Transition Economies." World Bank Regional and Sectoral Studies Series, Washington, DC.

Blaser, Jeremias, Dirk Besdziek, and Sarah Byrne. 2003. "Lessons Learned on Decentralization: A Literature Review." http://www.federalism.ch/files/categories/IRCC/.

Boadway, Robin. 2006. *Intergovernmental Fiscal Trans-*

fers: Principles and Practice. Washington, DC: World Bank.

Braathen, Einar, Amon Chaligha, and Odd-Helge Fjeldstad. 2005. "Local Governance, Finances and Service Delivery in Tanzania: A Summary of Findings from Six Councils." Joint Report of NIBR, CMI, and REPOA, Dar es Salaam, Tanzania.

Brosio, Giorgio. 2002. "An Evaluation of the World Bank Support for Decentralization in the Middle East and North Africa Countries of Algeria, Egypt, Morocco, Tunisia, West Bank." Background Paper for Independent Evaluation Group, World Bank, Washington, DC.

Center for Democracy and Governance. 2000. "Decentralization and Democratic Local Governance Programming Handbook." Technical Publication Series, CDG, Washington, DC.

Chattopadhyay, R., and Esther Duflo. 2004. "Impact of Reservation in Panchayati Raj: Evidence from a Nationwide Randomized Experiment." *Economic and Political Weekly* 39 (9): 979–86.

———. 2001. "Women as Policy Makers: Evidence from an India-Wide Randomized Policy Experiment." National Bureau of Economic Research Working Paper 8615. http://www.nber.org/papers/w8615.

Cheema, G. Shabbir, and Dennis A. Rondinelli, eds. 2007. *Decentralizing Governance: Emerging Concepts and Practices.* Washington, DC, and Boston, MA: Brookings Institution Press and Harvard University.

Crook, Richard, and Alan Sverrisson. 2001. "Decentralisation and Poverty-Alleviation in Developing Countries: A Comparative Analysis or Is West Bengal Unique?" Institute of Development Studies Working Paper 130, Brighton, U.K.

DEGE Consult and NCG (Nordic Consulting Group). 2006. "Survey on Support to Local Governance and Decentralization." For the Informal Donor Working Group on Local Governance and Decentralisation. http://www.euromedina.org/bibliotheque_fichiers/Doc_SurveyLocGovDec.pdf.

Devarajan, S., V. Swaroop, and H.F. Zou. 1998. "Fiscal Decentralization and Economic Growth: A Cross-Country Study." *Journal of Urban Economics,* 37 (2): 313–44.

Development Partners Working Group on Decentralization and Local Governance. 2007. "Alignment Strategies in the Field of Decentralisation and Local Governance: A Review of Country Practices and Experiences." Philippines Development Forum, Manila.

Dhimitri, Albana, Belinda Ikonomi, and Majlinda Dhuka. 2006. "Regional Development Policy Performance in Albania." Fiscal Decentralization Initiative for Central and Eastern Europe Paper, World Bank, Washington, DC.

Dickovick, J. Tyler. 2003. "Centralism and Decentralization." In *Unitary States: A Comparative Analysis of Peru and Senegal*, ed. J. Tyler Dickovick. Princeton, NJ: Princeton University.

Dillinger, William. 1994 "Decentralization and Its Implications for Service Delivery." Urban Management Institute Paper, World Bank, Washington, DC.

Dillinger, William, and Steven B. Webb. 1999. "Fiscal Management in Federal Democracies: Argentina and Brazil." Policy Research Working Paper 2121, World Bank, Washington, DC.

Dunn, Jonathan, and Deborah Wetzel. 1998. "Fiscal Decentralization in Former Socialist Economies: Progress and Prospects." Paper presented at NTA Conference, Atlanta.

Echeverri-Gent, John. 1993. *The State and the Poor: Public Policy and Political Development in India and the United States.* Berkeley: University of California Press.

Eskeland, G., and D. Filmer. 2002. "Autonomy, Participation, and Learning in Argentine Schools: Findings and Their Implications for Decentralization." Policy Research Working Paper 2766, World Bank, Washington, DC.

Evans, Anne, and Nick Manning. 2004. "Administrative Decentralization: A Review of Staffing Practices during Decentralization in Eight Countries." Draft Working Paper, World Bank, Washington, DC.

EU (European Commission). 2007. "Supporting Decentralization and Local Governance in Third Countries." Tools and Methods Series, Reference Document No. 2, Brussels.

Faguet, Jean-Paul. 2001. "Does Decentralization Increase Government Responsiveness to Local Needs? Evidence from Bolivia." Policy Research Working Paper 2516, World Bank, Washington, DC.

Faguet, Jean-Paul, and Fabio Sanchez. 2006. "Decentralization's Effects on Educational Outcomes in Bolivia and Colombia." LSE Research Online Working Paper, World Bank, Washington, DC.

Fanthorpe, Richard. 2006. "On the Limits of Liberal Peace: Chiefs and Democratic Decentralization in Post-War Sierra Leone." *African Affairs* 105 (418): 27–49.

Fernandez, Eduardo. 2007. "Assess Bank Support for Improving Governance, Including Capacity Building, Public Sector Reform and Decentralization." Background Paper for Independent Evaluation Group, World Bank, Washington, DC.

Fjeldstad, Odd-Helge, Einar Braathen, and Amon Chaligha. 2006. "Local Government Reform in Tanzania 2002–2005: Summary of Research Findings on Governance, Finance, and Service Delivery." *REPOA Brief* 6 (October) 1–8.

Fleiner, Thomas, and Flora Musonda. 2002 "Evaluating Bank Support for Improving Governance through Localization/Decentralization." Background Paper for Independent Evaluation Group, World Bank, Washington, DC.

Galiani, Sebastián, and Ernesto Schargrodsky. 2001."Evaluating the Impact of School Decentralization on Education Quality." http://www.utdt.edu/Upload/_115332118904928800.pdf.

Gershberg, Alec Ian. 1998. "Decentralization and Recentralization: Lessons from the Social Sectors in Mexico and Nicaragua." Working Paper No. 379, Inter-American Development Bank, Washington, DC.

Girishankar, Navin, David DeGroot, and T.V. Pillay. 2006. "Measuring Intergovernmental Fiscal Performance in South Africa: Issues in Municipal Grant Monitoring." Africa Region Working Paper Series No. 98, World Bank, Washington, DC.

Government of Albania and the World Bank. 2006. "Albania: Public Expenditure and Financial Accountability (PEFA) Public Financial Management Assessment." Working Paper No. 39483, World Bank, Washington, DC.

Government of Punjab (Pakistan) and the World Bank. 2005. "Islamic Republic of Pakistan: Punjab Public Financial Management and Accountability (PEFA) Assessment." South Asia Financial Management Report No. 32569-PAK, World Bank, Washington, DC.

Guadagni, Maurizio, Gabriela Boyer, Aidan Gulliver, Paola Perez-Alemán, and Dagoberto Rivera. 2000. "Local Governments and Sustainable Rural Development: Effects and Potential Sustainability of the Municipalities Project (Protierra) in Nicaragua." Sustainable Development Network Working Paper, World Bank, Washington, DC.

Hakielimu. 2005. *Three Years of PEDP Implementation: Key Findings from Government Reviews.* http://www. Hakielimu.org/ThreeYearsofPEDPImplementation2005.pdf.

Hauge, Arild. 2001. "Strengthening Capacity for Monitoring and Evaluation in Uganda: A Results-Based Management Perspective." ECD Working Series No. 8, World Bank, Washington, DC.

Hesselbarth, Susanne, Finn Hansen, and Hans Olsen. 2007. "Alignment Strategies in the Field of Decentralization and Local Governance: A Review of Country Practices and Experiences." International Development Partner Harmonization for Enhanced Aid Effectiveness and Development Partners Working Group on Local Governance and Decentralisation. Philippines Development Forum, Manila.

IADB (Inter-American Development Bank). 2001. "Summary of Findings—Decentralization and Effective Citizen Participation: Six Cautionary Tales." Office of Evaluation and Oversight Report RE-250, Inter-American Development Bank, Washington, DC.

———. 2000. "Subnational Development Strategy." Sustainable Development Department Strategy Paper, Inter-American Development Bank, Washington, DC.

IEG (Independent Evaluation Group). 2008. *Public Sector Reform: What Works and Why?* IEG Study Series. Washington, DC: World Bank.

———. 2007a. "Albania: Public Administration Reform Project." Implementation and Completion Report Review, World Bank, Washington, DC. http://wbln1023.worldbank.org/oed/oeddoclib.nsf/DocUNIDViewForJavaSearch/8525682E0068603785257305006 91A70?opendocument.

———. 2007b. "Country Financial Accountability Assessments and Country Procurement Assessment Reports: How Effective Are World Bank Fiduciary Diagnostics?" World Bank, Washington, DC.

———. 2007c. "An Evaluation of Bank Support for Decentralization and Strengthening Intergovernmental Relations." IEG Working Paper Series, World Bank, Washington, DC.

———. 2007d. "Evaluation of the World Bank's Assistance for Primary Education to Pakistan: A Country Case Study." IEG Working Paper Series, World Bank, Washington, DC.

———. 2007e. "Evaluation of the World Bank's Assistance for Primary Education to Peru: A Country Case Study." IEG Working Paper Series, World Bank, Washington, DC.

———. 2007f. "India Tamil Nadu Urban Project (Credit 1923-IND), Second Tamil Nadu Urban Development Project (Loan 4478-IND)." Project Performance Assessment Report, World Bank, Washington, DC.

———. 2007g. *The World Bank in Indonesia, 1999–2006: Country Assistance Evaluation.* Washington, DC: World Bank.

———. 2006a. *From Schooling Access to Learning Outcomes: An Unfinished Agenda—An Evaluation of World Bank Support to Primary Education.* IEG Study Series. Washington, DC: World Bank.

———. 2006b. *Madagascar: Country Assistance Evaluation.* Washington, DC: World Bank.

———. 2006c. *Pakistan: An Evaluation of the World Bank's Assistance.* IEG Study Series. Washington, DC: World Bank.

———. 2006d. *Republic of Yemen: Country Assistance Evaluation.* Washington, DC: World Bank.

———. 2006e. *Review of the Bank's Fiduciary Instruments: An OED Evaluation.* Washington, DC: World Bank.

———. 2005a. *Albania: Country Assistance Evaluation.* Washington, DC: World Bank.

———. 2005b. *The Effectiveness of World Bank Support for Community-Based and -Driven Development.* IEG Study Series. Washington, DC: World Bank.

———. 2004a. *Brazil: Forging a Strategic Partnership for Results. An OED Evaluation of World Bank Assistance.* Washington, DC: World Bank.

———. No date. "Progress Report 2000/01.The United Republic of Tanzania." http://povlibrary.worldbank.org/files/Tanzania_PRSP_ProgRep.pdf.

———. 2004c. *The World Bank's Assistance to Primary Education: An OED Portfolio Review.* Washington, DC: World Bank.

Institute of Development Studies. 2007. "Decentralizing Service Delivery?" ed. Mark Robinson, special issue. *IDS Bulletin* 38 (1).

Jeanrenaud, Claude. 2003. "Evaluation of World Bank Support for Decentralization in Sub-Saharan African Countries." IEG Background Paper, World Bank, Washington, DC.

Jette, Christian. 2005. "Democratic Decentralization and Poverty Reduction: The Bolivian Case." New York: United Nations Development Programme.

Jiminez, E., and Y. Sawada. 1999. "Do Community-Managed Schools Work? An Evaluation of El Salvador's EDUCO Program." *World Bank Economic Review* 13 (3): 415–41.

Jutting, Johannes, Céline Kauffmann, Ida McDonnell, Holger Osterrieder, Nicolas Pinaud, and Lucia Wegner. 2004. "Decentralization and Poverty in Developing Countries: Exploring the Impact." OECD-DAC Working Paper No. 236, Issy-les-Moulineaux, France.

Kaiser, Kai. 2006. "Decentralization Reforms." In *Analyzing the Distributional Impact of Reforms: A Practitioner's Guide to Pension, Health, Labor Market, Public Sector Downsizing, Taxation, Decentralization and Macroeconomic Modeling,* eds. Aline Coudouel and Stefano Paternostro, 313–54. Washington, DC: World Bank.

Katsiaouni, Olympios. 2003. "Decentralization and Poverty Reduction: Does it Work?" Paper presented at the Fifth Global Forum on Reinventing Government, Mexico City, November 3–7.

Khaleghian, Peyvand. 2003. "Decentralization and Public Services: The Case of Immunization." Policy Research Working Paper 2989, World Bank, Washington, DC.

King, E., and B. Ozler. 1998. "What's Decentralization Got to Do with Learning? The Case of Nicaragua's School Autonomy Reform." Working Paper, World Bank, Washington, DC.

Lakshminarayanan, R. 2003. "Decentralization and Its Implications for Reproductive Health: The Philippines Experience." *Reproductive Health Matters* 11 (21): 96–107.

Lamchovichina, Elena, Lili Liu, and Mohan Nagarajan. 2006. "Subnational Fiscal Sustainability Analysis: What Can We Learn from Tamil Nadu?" Policy Research Working Paper No. 3947, World Bank, Washington, DC.

Levy, Brian. 2004. "The Governance of Service Delivery in Europe and Central Asia." Working Paper No. 36141, World Bank, Washington, DC.

Lewis, Blane D. 2003. *Minimum Local Public Service Delivery Standards in Indonesia: Fiscal Implications and Affordability Concerns.* Research Triangle Park, NC: Research Triangle Institute International.

Litvack, Jennie, and Jessica Seddon. 1999. "Decentralization Briefing Notes." Working Paper, World Bank Institute, Washington, DC.

Mackay, Keith. 2007. *How to Build M&E Systems to Support Better Government.* Washington, DC: World Bank.

Mahar, Dennis J., and William R. Dillinger. 1983. "Financing State and Local Government in Brazil Recent Trends and Issues." Working Paper 612, World Bank, Washington, DC.

Manor, James. 2003. *Local Governance.* New Delhi, India: Swedish International Development Authority.

Marques, José, and Ian Bannon. 2003. "Central America: Education Reform in a Post-Conflict Setting—Opportunities and Challenges." CPR Working Paper No. 4, World Bank, Washington, DC.

Momoniat, Ismail. 2002. *Understanding Fiscal Decentralization in South Africa*. Washington, DC: World Bank.

OECD-DAC. 2004. "Lessons Learned on Donor Support to Decentralization and Local Governance." DAC Evaluation Series, OECD, Paris.

OECD Donor Working Group on Local Governance and Decentralization. 2006. *Survey on Support to Local Governance and Decentralization.* Oslo: Danish Environmental Cconsulting Group and Nordic Consulting Group.

Okidi, John A., and Madina Guloba. 2006. *Decentralization and Development Issues: Emerging Issues from Uganda's Experience.* Kampala, Uganda: Economic Policy Research Center.

Peterson, George E., and Particia Clarke Annez. 2007. *Financing Cities: Fiscal Responsibility and Urban Infrastructure in Brazil, China, India, Poland and South Africa.* New Delhi, India, and Washington, DC: Sage Publications and World Bank.

Prud'homme, Remy. 1995. "The Dangers of Decentralization." *World Bank Economic Observer* 10 (2): 201–20.

Raich, Uri. 2005. "Fiscal Determinants of Empowerment." Policy Research Working Paper No. 3705, World Bank, Washington, DC

REPOA. No date. "Is Government Managing Money Well? Findings from Recent Audit Reports." http://www.repoa.or.tz/tgn/index.php.

Reserve Bank of India. Various years. *State Finances—A Study of Budget.* Mumbai: Reserve Bank of India.

Rodden, Jonathan A., and Gunnar S. Eskeland. 2003. *Fiscal Decentralization and the Challenge of Hard Budget Constraints*. Cambridge, MA: MIT Press.

Rondinelli, Dennis, and Shabbir Cheema, eds. 2007. *Decentralizing Governance Emerging Concepts and Practices.* Washington, DC: Brookings Institution.

Saxena, N.C. 2003. "Issues in Panchayats." http://www.panchayats.org/downloads/Panchayats%20NC%20Sax.PDF.

Schneider, Aaron. 2003. "Who Gets What from Whom? The Impact of Decentralisation on Tax Capacity and Pro-Poor Policy." IDS Working Paper 179, Institute of Development Studies, Brighton, U.K.

Shah, Anwar, ed. 2006a. *Fiscal Management*. Public Sector Governance and Accountability Series. Washington, DC: World Bank.

———. 2006b. *Local Governance in Developing Countries: Public Sector Governance and Accountability Services.* Washington, DC: World Bank.

———. 2004. "Fiscal Decentralization in Developing and Transition Economies: Progress, Problems, and the Promise." Policy Research Working Paper Series 3282, World Bank, Washington, DC.

———. 1998. "Balance, Accountability, and Responsiveness Lessons about Decentralization." Policy Research Working Paper, World Bank, Washington, DC.

Smoke, Paul. 2001. "Fiscal Decentralization in Developing Countries: A Review of Current Concepts and Practice, Democracy." Governance and Human Rights Programme Paper Number 2, United Nations Research Institute for Social Development, New York.

Smoke, Paul, and Yun-Hwan Kim, eds. 2002. *Intergovernmental Fiscal Transfers in Asia: Current Practice and Challenges for the Future.* Manila: Asian Development Bank.

Spahn, Paul Bernd. 2002. "World Bank Support for Decentralization/Localization in the ECA Region—Second Report: Lessons Learned and Recommendations." Background Paper for Independent Evaluation Group, World Bank, Washington, DC.

Steiner, Susan. 2006. "Decentralization in Uganda: Exploring the Constraints for Poverty Reduction." German Institute of Global and Area Studies Working Paper No. 31, Hamburg.

Steinich, Markus. 2000. "Monitoring and Evaluating Support to Decentralization: Challenges and Dilemmas." Paper presented at European Support for Democratic Decentralization and Municipal Development—A Contribution to Local Development and Poverty Reduction, Maastricht, June 14–15.

Taliercio, Robert R. 2005. "Substantial Own-Source Revenue: Getting Policy and Administration Right." In *East Asia Decentralizes: Making Local Government Work*, 107–28. Washington, DC: World Bank.

Tanzi, V. 1996. "Fiscal Federalism and Decentralization: A Review of Some Efficiency and Macroeconomics Aspects." In *Annual World Bank Conference on Development Economics,* eds. M. Bruno and B. Pleskovic, 295–316. Washington, DC: World Bank.

Ter-Minassian, Teresa. 1997. *Fiscal Federalism in Theory and Practice*. Washington, DC: IMF.

Tidrick, Gene. 2007. "Bank Support for 'Pro-Poor' Growth and Investment Climate." Background Paper for Independent Evaluation Group, World Bank, Washington, DC.

Tommasi, Mariano. 2002. "Evaluation of World Bank Support for Decentralization in the LAC Region." Background Paper for Independent Evaluation Group, World Bank, Washington, DC.

United Nations. 2005. *UN Poverty Report.* New York: United Nations.

United Nations Economic and Social Council. 2005. "Decentralization for Poverty Reduction." Paper presented at meeting of Economic and Social Commission for Asia and the Pacific: Committee on Poverty Reduction, Bangkok, Thailand, November 23–25.

UN-Habitat. 2007. *International Guidelines on Decentralization and the Strengthening of Local Authorities.* New York: United Nations.

United Republic of Tanzania. 2007. "Local Government Reform Program—Embedding Decentralization by Devolution across the Government." Main Assessment Report, Prime Minister's Office, Regional Administration and Local Government, Dodoma.

———. 2005. "Local Government Fiscal Review." President's Office, Regional Administration and Local Government & Ministry of Finance.

United Republic of Tanzania, International Monetary Fund, and World Bank. 1999. "Tanzania Enhanced Structural Adjustment Facility Policy Framework Paper for 1998/99–2000/01." World Bank, Washington, DC.

USAID (United States Agency for International Development). 2006. *Assessing the Impact of Devolution on Healthcare and Education in Pakistan.* Washington, DC: The Urban Institute.

———. 2006. "Stocktaking on Indonesia's Recent Decentralization Reforms—Summary Report." Washington, DC: USAID.

———. 2000. *Decentralization and Democratic Local Governance Programming Handbook.* Technical Publication Series. Washington, DC: Center for Democracy and Governance.

van Zyl, Johan, Tulio Barbosa, Andrew N. Parker, and Loretta Sonn. 1995. "A Case Study from Northeast Brazil." Policy Research Working Paper 1498, World Bank, Washington, DC.

Vedeld, Trond. 2003. "Democratic Decentralization and Poverty Reduction: Exploring the Linkages." Forum for Development Studies. Oslo: Norwegian Institute of International Affairs.

Verheijen, Tony. 2007. "Administrative Capacity in the EU Member States: The Limits of Innovation?" World Bank Working Paper No. 40559, World Bank, Washington, DC.

von Braun, Joachim, and Ulrike Grote. 2000. "Does Decentralization Serve the Poor?" Paper presented at the IMF Conference on Fiscal Decentralization, Washington, DC, November 20–21.

Webb, Steven B. 2004. "Fiscal Responsibility Laws for Subnational Discipline: The Latin American Experience." Policy Research Working Paper 3309, World Bank, Washington, DC.

Weber-Venghaus, Svenja. 2007. "Bank Assistance to Education, Health and Gender in Ethiopia." Background Paper for Independent Evaluation Group, World Bank, Washington, DC.

Wetzel, Deborah. 2001. "Decentralization in the Transition Economies: Challenges and the Road Ahead." Working Paper, World Bank, Washington, DC.

Wiesner, Eduardo. 2003. "Bank Lending for Subnational Development: The Policy and Institutional Challenges." IADB Office of Evaluation and Oversight Working Paper Series, Washington, DC.

Winkler, Donald R. 2005. *Understanding Decentralization.* Washington, DC: USAID.

Winkler, Donald, and Alec Ian Gershberg. 2000. "Education Decentralization in Latin America: The Effects on the Quality of Schooling." LCSHD Paper Series No. 59, World Bank, Washington, DC.

World Bank. 2007a. "Burkina Faso: Seventh Poverty Reduction Support Credit Project." Project Information Document No. AB2729, World Bank, Washington, DC.

———. 2007b. "Decentralization and Local Governance in MENA: A Survey of Policies, Institutions, and Practices—A Review of Decentralization Experience in Eight Middle East and North Africa Countries."

———. 2007c. "Education Sector Strategy Update." http://web.worldbank.org/WBSITE/EXTERNAL/TOPICS/EXTEDUCATION/0,contentMDK:20262538~menuPK:282402~pagePK:148956~piPK:216618~theSitePK:282386,00.html.

———. 2007d. "Healthy Development: The World Bank Strategy for Health, Nutrition, and Population Results." Board Report No. 39485, World Bank, Washington, DC.

———. 2007e. "Implementation Plan for Strengthening World Bank Group Engagement on Governance and

Anti-Corruption." Operations Policy and Country Services (SecM2007-0425), World Bank, Washington, DC.

———. 2007f. "Local Government Discretion and Accountability: A Local Governance Framework." Social Development Department in collaboration with the Finance, Economics and Urban Department and the Social Protection Team. Forthcoming.

———. 2007g. "Morocco Municipal Finance Project II." Implementation Completion Report, World Bank, Washington, DC.

———. 2007h. "Pakistan—Balochistan Province: Public Financial Management and Accountability Assessment." Integrative Fiduciary Assessment No. 39764, World Bank, Washington, DC.

———. 2007i. "Pakistan—Northwest Frontier Province: Public Financial Management and Accountability Assessment." Integrative Fiduciary Assessment No. 39759, World Bank, Washington, DC.

———. 2007j. "Pakistan—Punjab Province: Public Financial Management and Accountability Assessment." Integrative Fiduciary Assessment No. 39761, World Bank, Washington, DC.

———. 2007k. "Russia Education Reform Project." Implementation Completion and Results Report No. ICR0000393, World Bank, Washington, DC.

———. 2007l. "Strengthening the World Bank Engagement on Governance and Anticorruption." Report No. 39055, World Bank, Washington, DC.

———. 2007m. "Toward High-Quality Education in Peru: Standards, Accountability, and Capacity Building." World Bank Country Study No. 40557, World Bank, Washington, DC.

———. 2006a. "Albania Health Sector Note." Report No. 32612, World Bank, Washington, DC.

———. 2006b. "Bolivia: Towards an Inclusive Decentralization." Institutional and Governance Review No. 36285, World Bank, Washington, DC.

———. 2006c. "Bolivia: Towards a New Social Contract: Options for the Constituent Assembly." Social Analysis No. 38271, World Bank, Washington, DC.

———. 2006d. "Bosnia and Herzegovina: Addressing Fiscal Challenges and Enhancing Growth Prospects." Public Expenditure and Institutional Review, World Bank, Washington, DC.

———. 2006e. "Brief Local Government Reform in Tanzania 2002–2005: Summary of Research Findings in Governance and Service Delivery." World Bank, Washington, DC.

———. 2006f. "Colombia: Municipal Development and Urban Infrastructure Services Development Projects." Project Performance Assessment Report No. 36435, World Bank, Washington, DC.

———. 2006g. *Making Services Work for the Poor in Indonesia: Focusing on Achieving Results on the Ground.* Washington, DC: World Bank.

———. 2006h. "Pakistan: Second Development Policy Credit Project." Implementation Completion and Results Report No. 35465, World Bank, Washington, DC.

———. 2006i. "Philippines: National Program Support for Basic Education Project." Project Appraisal Document No. 35445-PH, World Bank, Washington, DC.

———. 2006j. "Philippines: Support for Strategic Local Development and Investment Project." Project Appraisal Document No. 36317, World Bank, Washington, DC.

———. 2006k. "Tanzania Public Expenditure and Financial Accountability Review, Local Government Fiscal Review—FY05." Report No. 36642-TZ, World Bank, Washington, DC.

———. 2006l. "Tanzania: Public Expenditure Review." Local Goernment Fiduciary Assessment from the Annual Consultative Meeting, Dar es Salaam, May 12–13.

———. 2005a. "Albania: Health System Recovery and Development Project." Implementation Completion and Results Report No. 32718, World Bank, Washington, DC.

———. 2005b. "Bosnia and Herzegovina: Transition Assistance Credit, Public Finance Structural Adjustment First and Second Credits, and Social Sector Adjustment Credit Projects." Project Performance Assessment Report No. 31343, World Bank, Washington, DC.

———. 2005c. *East Asia Decentralizes: Making Local Government Work*. Washington, DC: World Bank.

———. 2005d. "Empowering People by Transforming Institutions: Social Development in World Bank Operations." Board Report No. 31494, World Bank, Washington, DC.

———. 2005e. "Fiscal Costs of Structural Reforms." Public Expenditure Review No. 30741, World Bank, Washington, DC.

———. 2005f. "Philippines: Economic and Sector Work on Decentralization." Working Paper, World Bank, Washington, DC.

———. 2005g. "Reforming Public Institutions and Strengthening Governance: A World Bank Strategy,

Implementation Update: FY05." Public Sector Governance Board Report, World Bank, Washington, DC.

———. 2005h. "Russia: Fiscal Costs of Structural Reforms." Public Expenditure Review No. 30741, World Bank, Washington, DC.

———. 2005i."Subnational Policy Lending." Good Practice Note for Development Policy Lending, World Bank, Washington, DC.

———. 2005j. "What Determines the Extent of Fiscal Decentralization? The Russian Paradox." Policy Research Working Paper No. WPS3710, World Bank, Washington, DC.

———. 2004a. "Assessment Report on Minimum Conditions and Performance Measures of Local Government Authorities, Sikonge District Council." President's Office, Regional Administration and Local Government, LGSP.

———. 2004b. "Bolivia—Second Programmatic Structural Adjustment Credit for Decentralization." Implementation Completion and Results Report No. 31034, World Bank, Washington, DC.

———. 2004c. *Decentralization in Madagascar.* Washington, DC: World Bank.

———. 2004d. "Designing Development Policy Operations." Good Practice Note for Development Policy Lending, World Bank, Washington, DC.

———. 2004e. "Education Decentralization and Accountability Relationships in Latin America." Policy Research Working Paper 3453, World Bank, Washington, DC.

———. 2004f. "Morocco: Basic Education Project." Implementation Completion Report, World Bank, Washington, DC.

———. 2004g. "Philippines—Decentralization in the Philippines: Strengthening Local Government Financing and Resource Management in the Short Term." Public Sector Study Report No. 26104, World Bank, Washington, DC.

———. 2004h. "Review of Fiscal Developments and Budget Management Issues FY03–FY04. Joint Evaluation Report." Report presented at the Public Expenditure Review FY04 Consultative Meeting, Dar es Salaam, May 14.

———. 2004i. "Uganda: Local Government Development Program." Implementation Completion Report No. 30284, World Bank, Washington, DC.

———. 2004j. *World Development Report: Making Services Work for Poor People.* Washington, DC: World Bank.

———. 2003a. "Morocco—Second Municipal Finance Project." Implementation Completion and Results Report No. 26153, World Bank, Washington, DC.

———. 2003b. "Nicaragua—Poverty Reduction Strategy Paper and Joint IDA-IMF Assessment: Second Annual Progress Report." Poverty Reduction Strategy Report No. 27500, World Bank, Washington, DC.

———. 2003c. "Reaching the Rural Poor: A Renewed Strategy for Rural Development." Working Paper No. 30411, World Bank, Washington, DC.

———. 2003d. "Sustaining Forests: A World Bank Strategy." World Bank Strategy Paper No. 35535, World Bank, Washington, DC.

———. 2003e. *Water Resources Sector Strategy. Strategic Directions for World Bank Engagement.* Washington, DC: World Bank. http://siteresources.worldbank.org/INTINFNETWORK/Resources/water.pdf.

———. 2002. "Brazil: Issues in Fiscal Federalism." Report No. 22523-BR. World Bank. Washington, DC.

———. 2001a. "Decentralization and Governance: Does Decentralization Improve Public Service Delivery?" PREM Notes No. 55, World Bank, Washington, DC.

———. 2001b. *Making Sustainable Commitments: An Environmental Strategy for the World Bank.* Washington, DC: World Bank.

———. 2001c. "Morocco Country Assistance Strategy." Report No. 22115, World Bank, Washington, DC.

———. 2001d. "Peru Institutional Governance Review," Report No. 22637, World Bank, Washington, DC.

———. 2001e. "Tanzania: Public Expenditure Review." Report No. 22078, World Bank, Washington, DC.

———. 2000a. *Cities in Transition: World Bank Urban and Local Government Strategy.* Washington, DC: World Bank.

———. 2000b. "Pakistan: Reforming the Provincial Finances in the Context of Devolution—An Eight-Point Agenda." PREM Working Paper No. 21362, World Bank, Washington, DC.

———. 2000c. *Reforming Public Institutions and Strengthening Governance: A World Bank Strategy.* Washington, DC: World Bank.

———. 1999a. "Education Sector Strategy Paper." Sector Strategy Paper, World Bank, Washington, DC.

———. 1999b. "Philippines: The Challenge of Economic Recovery." Sector Report No. 18895, World Bank, Washington, DC.

———. 1998a. "Building Institutions and Financing Local Development: Lessons from Brazil and the Philippines. Municipal Development Project in the State of

Parana (Loan 3100-BR) Municipal Development Project in the State of Rio Grande do Sul (Loan 31 29-BR) Municipal Development Project in the Philippines (Loan 2435-PH) Second Municipal Development Project in the Philippines (Loan 3146-PHI)." Report No. 18727, World Bank, Washington, DC.

———. 1998b. "Rethinking Decentralization in Developing Countries." Poverty Reduction and Economic Management Report, World Bank, Washington, DC.

———. 1997a. "Health, Nutrition and Population." Sector Strategy Paper No. 17092. Washington, DC, World Bank.

———. 1997b. *World Development Report: The State in a Changing World*. Washington, DC: World Bank.

———. 1994a. "Fiscal Decentralization and Intergovernmental Finances in the Republic of Albania." Policy Research Working Paper No. WPS1384, World Bank, Washington, DC.

———. 1994b. "Philippines—Devolution and Health Services: Managing Risks and Opportunities." Sector Report No. 12343, World Bank, Washington, DC.

———. 1992a. "Brazil: The Challenge of Municipal Sector Development in the 1990s. Volume l: Policy Summary and Reform Proposals." LAI Department Infrastructure Operations Division Latin America and the Caribbean Regional Office, World Bank, Washington, DC.

———. 1992b. "Public Sector Debt, Fiscal Deficits, and Economic Adjustment: A Comparative Study of Six EMENA Countries." Policy Research Working Paper No. WPS840, World Bank, Washington, DC.

Wunsch, James S. 2005. "Decentralization, Local Governance and the Democratic Transition in Southern Africa: A Comparative Analysis." *African Studies Quarterly*.